205-1068

INSTANT APPLAUSE

INSTANT APPLAUSE

26
very short
complete plays

Blizzard Publishing • Winnipeg

Instant Applause: 26 Very Short Complete Plays
first published 1994 by
Blizzard Publishing Inc.
73 Furby St., Winnipeg, Canada R3C 2A2
© 1994 Copyright remains with the authors.
Reprinted 1997.

Cover art by Linda Mullin.
Printed in Canada by Friesens Printing.

Published with the assistance of
the Canada Council and the Manitoba Arts Council.

Canadian Cataloguing in Publication Data

Main entry under title:
  Instant applause
  ISBN 0-921368-34-8
  1. One-act plays, Canadian (English)*
  2. Canadian drama (English) — 20th century.*
  PS8309.0515 1994   C812'.04108054   C94-920035-2
  PR9196.7.0515 1994

Contents

Air-Talk

by Carol Shields

Characters

Two men, A and B; A is middle-aged.

Setting

The scene is the interior of a small aircraft just before take-off.
Two side-by-side seats are angled toward the audience.

> *(A enters carrying a bag with a tennis racquet. He checks his
> boarding pass, then checks his seat number.)*

A: Six-A.

> *(Turning to the audience, speaking with satisfaction.)*

I prefer a window seat.

> *(He stows his bag, with the tennis racquet protruding, under his
> seat, and then sits. B comes up behind him, also carrying a bag
> with a tennis racquet. He examines his ticket, then speaks to the
> audience in identical tones.)*

B: I prefer a window seat. Or, failing that—an aisle seat.

> *(He stows his bag, also with the tennis racquet protruding, under
> his seat, and then sits. The men perform movements in mirror*

image: they pull their seats forward, do up their seat belts, mime take-off motions, and cross their legs. The sound of motors, take-off noises, and then leveling off, are made by the men themselves, humming in unison.)

A: *(Striking up conversation.)* Tennis racquet, I see.

B: Yes.

A: Symbol or gesture?

B: Or both. Or neither.

A: Leitmotif of all you have formerly scorned or failed to earn?

B: Let's forget the tennis racquet. A contemplative life doesn't lend itself to momentary fleeting reductions.

A: Desires, you mean?

B: Desire is not a word in my vocabulary. I desire, you desire, he, she or it desires. Desire is an embarrassment. Wide open mouths. Third rate films.

A: How about the passive form? To be desired?

B: Better. The object of desire is innocent or can be.

A: Can be, indeed?

(They look at each other.)

B: Like Joanna? *(Looks away.)*

A: Who?

B: Imagine playing a game of tennis with Joanna. A hard sunny fall morning? One of those red clay courts? Joanna in white shorts and striped T-shirt?

A: I cannot imagine inviting Joanna for a game of tennis.

B: Why not? Let's be speculative. Let's give a little air to these narrow certainties of yours.

A: For one thing, I don't ... know how to play tennis. *(Gestures feebly at racquet, shrugs foolishly.)* I've never had the opportunity to ...

B: Go on.

A: And Joanna's psyche is so rotted out by therapy that she'd probably interpret an invitation to play tennis as ... as a hostile gesture.

B: Have you noticed ... somehow—and I'm sure you have—that very few people use the term "psyche" these days. It's one of those key generation words that attached to those who are over, say, the age of, well, fifty-five?

A: I am fifty-five, and have never pretended otherwise.

B: Even to Joanna?

A: I told her I had passed my fiftieth birthday. She told me she had passed her twentieth. We left it at that.

B: Tone of voice?

A: I beg your pardon?

B: Can you recall her tone of voice? When you had this discussion?

A: Knowing, candid, sensual. She is someone who is, always I suspect, in her imagination, a voluptuary. She gave that silky laugh of hers. This was after class, in the corridor.

B: Was this the same day she referred to your article on Pushkin?

A: She'd come across it in a journal. Browsing in the library, she said. Just stumbled across it.

B: You believe that?

A: No.

B: So there you were, in the corridor. The walls smeared with graffiti. She was leaning toward you slightly, listening hard, wearing a yellow sweater, her little white teeth. She asked you about Pushkin?

A: No, we'd finished with Pushkin.

B: Well then?

A: She had a poem to show me. She wanted my ...

B: Your ...?

A: My comments.

B: One of the Russian poets?

A: No, her own. Her poem. She pushed it into my hand.

B: Was it typewritten? Longhand? Describe it?

A: It's difficult to—

B: Try.

A: Lined paper, three-holed, felt pen.

B: Colour of ink?

A: This was some time ago—I don't know if I can recall the colour of the—

B: Pink?

A: More of a violet.

B: That disappointed you?

A: Yes, but charmed me also.

B: And the poem itself?

A: Not bad, not good. An I-spy-with-my-little-eye poem—the universe-in-a-grain-of-sand sort of thing—pretentious but somehow intimate. I told her I'd read it and give her my comments.

B: Hmmm.

A: What did you say?

B: I said, "Hmmmm." It's spelled with an H followed by a little family of Ms.

A: Haven't we ... met?

> *(They look at each other. From this point on, the two men's movements follow each other precisely, rather than in mirror image.)*

B: *(Looking away.)* A while back I was at a party and you were there. Joanna was there too, if I'm not mistaken. And you said something so ... so wise. About men and women, their ... predicament, the distance that separates them. I was impressed.

A: You're sure it was me? Not one of my colleagues?

B: It absolutely was you. I remember the impact of what you said, but not the actual line.

A: Wise, you say? Not wisecracking?

B: Wise. That's what impressed me.

A: You're certain you can't remember? It may be the only wise thing I ever said. About men and women, you say.

B: I was bowled over—

A: It's too bad you didn't write it down. Maybe someone else was there who remembers—

B: We were the only ones. Just the two of us. In a corner by the piano—

A: I thought you said Joanna was there.

B: In the room, I said. Not in our little corner by the—

A: She might have overheard. I could ask her if she—

B: She was talking to someone else. A very intense conversation, it looked like. You know how her elbow sort of ... flips out sideways when she gets intense. I couldn't help noticing ... that elbow, her left elbow, out.

A: And who exactly—

B: She was saying something about … of course, I only heard every fourth word.

A: About?

B: Jean-Paul Sartre, I think. That's what came floating over the hubbub.

A: Hubbub? One hardly ever hears of a hubbub these days.

B: More of a babble, but, yes, definitely the words: Jean-Paul Sartre.

A: Anything else?

B: About … something about some poems she'd written. She wondered if he—the man she was speaking so intently with, to, at—she wondered if he could find a few minutes to cast an eye over—

A: Large man? Small? Medium-sized?

B: Hard to say, hard to say.

A: I don't know why it should be so hard to say.

B: Wiry individual. That's what I'd say if I had to say something—I'd say wiry. Tennis player type.

> *(They look at each other. They begin to make motor sounds again, humming.)*

A: We're coming down.

B: You're not frightened, are you?

> *(Motor sounds continue; the plane is descending.)*

A: Not frightened, of course not.

B: Good fellow.

A: What about you? Nervous? Butterflies?

B: I'd feel better if … if she was here.

A: Joanna?

B: She did have these soft … pink … hands.

A: Pink, yes, Joanna's pink hands.

B: I wish you wouldn't say her name. Out loud like that.

A: Sorry.

B: Someone might—

> *(They continue to make motor noises, louder now.)*

A: This is the worst part, the last few minutes when the air pressure—

B: Here. Take my hand, why don't you?

(They hold hands briefly, shutting their eyes.)

A: That's ... better. Actually, you have a remarkable grip. For a man of fifty-five—

B: Almost there.

(They make the prolonged sound of a landing aircraft, followed by silence.)

A: *(Briskly, undoing his seat belt.)* Excellent flight. *(Rising, picking up his bag.)* Excellent!

B: First rate. *(Rises, picking up his bag, he gestures at A's tennis racquet.)* Tennis racquet, I see.

A: Never travel without my tennis racquet.

B: Never travel without—

A: Never travel, never never travel.

B: Never, never.

A: Never.

(Fade to black. The end.)

Wake

by David Widdicombe

Characters

ELLEN: In her forties.
CHLOE: Fifteen or sixteen.

Setting

The small entrance hall of a rather large house, perhaps with a staircase. There are flowers everywhere, covering everything—almost as if some demented florist was left alone for a few days to wreck his own special form of botanical havoc. Other than flowers, the set consists of a few fold-up chairs placed there for the evening, a small table with a vase filled with still more flowers, and maybe off to one corner a coat-rack laden with winter coats and scarves. It is night. A wake is in progress in the other rooms. Although the evening is semi-formal, none of the characters should give the impression they are the least bit wealthy. They are expected to look much better than they are able—and as a result, end up looking a little tacky.

(ELLEN is sitting on one of the chairs sobbing uncontrollably. There are three boxes of tissues sitting in her lap and a multitude of discarded tissues on the floor near her feet. She spends a lot of

13

time wiping her eyes and blowing her nose. A few minutes pass. Then CHLOE enters, slightly confused and lost, carrying a large plate of food. She decides to sit down. She then stares at ELLEN as though watching a very interesting movie. Long pause.)

CHLOE: I thought it was kinda beautiful.

ELLEN: *(Sniffling.)* What?

CHLOE: The thing.

ELLEN: What thing?

CHLOE: The whada-ya-callit. The service. I thought it was kinda beautiful. *(Pause.)* Especially the flowers. *(Pause.)* Know why they have flowers at funerals?

ELLEN: *(Sniffling.)* Huh?

CHLOE: I said, do ya know why they have flowers at funerals?

ELLEN: Decoration?

CHLOE: Most people think that. But they're really there ta kill the smell.

ELLEN: The smell?

CHLOE: You know. The smell of death.

ELLEN: I didn't know it had a smell.

CHLOE: Well it does. It's kinda like Vick's Vapo Rub. *(Beat.)* Or maybe sour milk—I can't remember.

(Pause. ELLEN continues to sob.)

CHLOE: I thought the make-up was good too.

ELLEN: They made him look like Bela Lugosi.

CHLOE: Who?

ELLEN: Dracula.

CHLOE: The vampire?

ELLEN: There's another Dracula?

CHLOE: I don't know.

ELLEN: He was wearin' blue eye shadow. Since when does a man wear blue eye shadow?

CHLOE: All the corpses I ever saw always had blue eye shadow. Men and women.

ELLEN: My Zachary did not wear blue eye shadow.

CHLOE: Oh God. You're not family, are ya?

ELLEN: I'm the widow.

CHLOE: Jesus.

(CHLOE quickly moves to a chair further away.)

ELLEN: Whatsa matter?

CHLOE: I'm not supposed ta talk ta family.

ELLEN: Why not?

CHLOE: I'm just not. Please don't make me talk to you.

ELLEN: Did Marybeth put you up to this?

CHLOE: Who's Marybeth?

ELLEN: My sister-in-law. The so-called hostess of this so-called wake.

CHLOE: This her house?

ELLEN: Yeah.

CHLOE: It's nice.

ELLEN: It doesn't always look like this. It's usually a regular pigsty. I can prove it. I have pictures.

CHLOE: Is she the one with the flaming red hair that kept squirmin' in her seat?

ELLEN: That's her. She never could sit still for more than five minutes.

CHLOE: And halfway through the service she whacked that poor little midget over the head with a prayer book.

ELLEN: That was her husband.

CHLOE: That midget was her husband?

ELLEN: He isn't a midget.

CHLOE: Sure looked like a midget. Just like the one I saw in a circus once—only that one seemed a lot happier and was wearin' shoes shaped like bananas—

ELLEN: Roy isn't a midget. He just has stunted growth.

CHLOE: I'll say.

ELLEN: He paid for all this.

CHLOE: What?

ELLEN: The funeral, the flowers, everythin'. He paid for it.

CHLOE: Geez. He must be rich.

ELLEN: He should be. He owns three Dairy Queens.

CHLOE: Three?

ELLEN: Who woulda thought a house like this could be built with
   ice cream.

CHLOE: It's nice.

ELLEN: What?

CHLOE: This house. It's nice.

ELLEN: Mmm.

   (Pause.)

CHLOE: What did your husband do? I mean before he died.

ELLEN: Who—Zachary?

CHLOE: Yeah.

ELLEN: He sold shoes.

CHLOE: Shoes?

ELLEN: Shoes.

CHLOE: What kinda shoes?

ELLEN: Shoe shoes.

CHLOE: Shoe shoes?

ELLEN: Shoe shoes.

CHLOE: You mean like brown shoes?

ELLEN: Brown shoes, black shoes, white shoes. Plain, everyday boring
   shoes shoes.

CHLOE: Oh. *(Long pause.)* You want a deviled egg?

ELLEN: No.

CHLOE: They're real good.

ELLEN: I hate deviled eggs.

CHLOE: These ones are real mayonaissey.

ELLEN: No thank you.

CHLOE: Whatta ya suppose the little eyes are?

ELLEN: What?

CHLOE: Somebody put little eyes on the eggs.

ELLEN: That's sick.

CHLOE: I think it's kinda cute. Maybe I shouldn't eat it.

ELLEN: Suit yourself.

   (Pause.)

CHLOE: You want a piece of celery?

ELLEN: No.

CHLOE: You don't like celery?

ELLEN: I'm not hungry, okay?

CHLOE: You would be if ya saw all the food they got in there. There's crackers and fifty million kinds of cheese and Fritos and pickles and potato salad and rolled-up baloney and celery and spaceship radishes and onion dip and pretzels and cheese dreams and little shrimps and little jam-cakes and lotsa little things with toothpicks stickin' in 'em. And they've even got a great big bucket of chicken from the Colonel. I love the Colonel, don't you?

ELLEN: For someone with a rampant fascination with food you certainly don't look very fat.

CHLOE: I don't?

ELLEN: No, you don't.

CHLOE: Gosh. I hope I don't have a tapeworm.

(She starts munching on a stalk of celery, pondering the thought. Pause.)

ELLEN: Do you haveta do that?

CHLOE: Do what?

ELLEN: Munch.

CHLOE: I always munch when I'm thinkin'.

ELLEN: Well it's gettin' on my nerves.

CHLOE: *(Pause.)* Sorry.

(Long pause.)

ELLEN: Don't stare at me.

CHLOE: I wasn't.

ELLEN: You were. You were starin' at me.

CHLOE: I wasn't. Honest.

(Pause.)

ELLEN: You think I should be in there with the others, don'tcha?

CHLOE: No.

ELLEN: Go ahead. Admit it. You think I should be in there.

CHLOE: Well—I don't know. Maybe. I guess. I don't know.

ELLEN: What the hell do you know.

CHLOE: I mean you bein' his wife and all.

ELLEN: I don't wanta go in there.

CHLOE: Why not?

ELLEN: I just don't.

CHLOE: All your family's in there.

ELLEN: They're not my family. They're his family and they all hate me.

CHLOE: How do you know?

ELLEN: Believe me. I know.

CHLOE: They're havin' a real good party.

ELLEN: I'm sure they are.

CHLOE: Your sister-in-law seemed pretty happy.

ELLEN: Probably drunk.

CHLOE: Think so?

ELLEN: Woman drinks like a sieve. I have pictures of that, too.

CHLOE: Maybe you'd feel better if ya got stinkin' drunk.

ELLEN: I don't wanta get stinkin' drunk.

CHLOE: My Daddy always says the best way ta overcome grief is ta get stinkin' drunk.

ELLEN: What does he know about grief?

CHLOE: Well he's seen a lot of it. So I guess he knows a lot.

ELLEN: Your Daddy knew my Zachary?

CHLOE: Sort of.

ELLEN: Whatta ya mean sort of?

CHLOE: My Daddy was the one that put the blue eye shadow on him.

ELLEN: What?

CHLOE: He's the mortician.

(Pause.)

ELLEN: Oh God. I'm talkin' ta the mortician's daughter.

CHLOE: That's me.

ELLEN: Just what the hell do you think you're doin' here?

CHLOE: I was invited.

ELLEN: By who?

CHLOE: My Daddy.

ELLEN: Since when does the mortician invite people ta my husband's wake?

CHLOE: You're not mad, are ya?

ELLEN: Why would I be mad? Just because you've got absolutely nothing ta do with this doesn't mean you don't deserve ta be here.

CHLOE: You are mad.

ELLEN: Look, I'm an emotional mess. I don't wanta waste my feelings talkin' ta someone that doesn't care.

CHLOE: I care.

ELLEN: You care?

CHLOE: Yeah.

ELLEN: You didn't even know him.

CHLOE: Doesn't mean I don't care.

ELLEN: You're just sayin' that so you can keep eating your free meal.

CHLOE: I am not.

ELLEN: You are.

CHLOE: I am not. I'm sayin' it 'cause I mean it.

ELLEN: Yeah, sure.

CHLOE: This isn't the first funeral I've been to you know.

ELLEN: I suppose you're gonna say they're all the same.

CHLOE: No—they're different, every single one. I know. I sit through a lotta funerals.

ELLEN: Whatta ya do—rate them on a scale of ten?

CHLOE: Mostly I just try ta meet boys.

ELLEN: At funerals?

CHLOE: I don't get out much.

ELLEN: Really.

CHLOE: Daddy doesn't let me.

ELLEN: You must go somewhere.

CHLOE: Well—sometimes he'll take me out ta dinner or sometin'. Usually the Colonel or the A&W. Anyplace where we don't haveta get outta the car. Daddy doesn't really know how ta relate ta livin' people, just dead ones.

ELLEN: He sounds like a real laugh riot.

CHLOE: But sometimes I get really angry that he doesn't let me outta the house—so ya know what I do ta get back at him?

ELLEN: I'm afraid ta ask.

CHLOE: I puke.

ELLEN: You what?

CHLOE: I puke. I shove my fingers down my throat and I puke. I puke in the kitchen, I puke in the living room—wherever I happen ta be at the time.

ELLEN: Don'tcha think that's a little drastic?

CHLOE: Not if I get my message across.

ELLEN: When I got angry at Zachary I just threw things.

CHLOE: That's too basic. Guys like ta watch things flyin' through the air. You wanta get their attention ya gotta puke right in fronta them.

ELLEN: I'll try ta remember that.

CHLOE: *(Changing subject.)* What's your name?

ELLEN: Ellen.

CHLOE: Like Ellen of Troy?

ELLEN: Huh?

CHLOE: Ellen of Troy, the one with the wooden horse.

ELLEN: That was Helen, not Ellen.

CHLOE: *(Disappointed.)* Oh. *(Pause.)* Don'tcha wanta know what my name is?

ELLEN: What is it?

CHLOE: Guess.

ELLEN: I don't wanta guess.

CHLOE: It starts with "C."

ELLEN: I don't wanta guess.

CHLOE: Chloe.

ELLEN: Chloe?

CHLOE: Short for chloroform.

ELLEN: You gotta be kidding.

CHLOE: Well I don't know for sure. But I have my suspicions.

ELLEN: That you were named after chloroform?

CHLOE: It was either that or formaldehyde.

ELLEN: That is the dumbest thing I've ever heard.

CHLOE: You don't know my Daddy.

ELLEN: I'm surprised your mother put up with it.

CHLOE: She didn't really have much say in it. She died when I was born.

ELLEN: What?

CHLOE: When I was born she died.

> *(Pause.)*

ELLEN: I'm sorry. I had no idea.

CHLOE: It's okay. I'm a bit of a jinx when it comes ta dying.

ELLEN: A jinx?

CHLOE: Yeah. First Mom, then Elvis.

ELLEN: Elvis?

CHLOE: Elvis died on my birthday.

ELLEN: No.

CHLOE: Yeah. Just up and died.

ELLEN: Well it was really his own fault.

CHLOE: I know.

ELLEN: What was it he died of?

CHLOE: Hot peppers.

ELLEN: No, I think it was pills or sometin'.

CHLOE: Hot peppers.

ELLEN: Elvis did not die of hot peppers.

CHLOE: He choked on one.

ELLEN: He did not.

CHLOE: He did. I was right there.

ELLEN: Elvis?

CHLOE: Elvis.

ELLEN: The king of rock and roll.

CHLOE: The cat.

ELLEN: The cat?

CHLOE: We found him one summer out by the back porch. He was real scrawny—had bones like chicken-bones. I used ta give him a saucer of milk and whatever scraps we had—forgot ta feed him one time 'cause it was my birthday and he jumped up on the kitchen table and started wolfin' down some chicken gumbo filled with hot peppers— I thought he was gonna burn his little tongue off but he didn't—he just choked.

ELLEN: You fed hot peppers to a cat?

CHLOE: I didn't feed him. He was feedin' himself.

ELLEN: Was he sick?

CHLOE: He died, didn't he? *(Pause.)* I guess you think that's kinda morbid, huh?

ELLEN: Kinda.

CHLOE: I got lotsa death stories. Elvis choking on a pepper is my favourite. It's sad, but it's my favourite.

(Pause.)

ELLEN: I'm fourteen and I'm ridin' in this pick-up bein' driven by my Uncle John D. I'm in the back with my cousin Richie and a coupla bales of hay—we're comin' back from town and Richie is teasin' me by moonin' the farms and darin' me ta do the same. So ta prove I'm not some weakling dumb girl I start moonin' the farms too. We moon the cows, we moon the mailboxes. After a while it gets so funny it's painful. We can't stop laughin' and cryin'. Then all of a sudden Uncle John yells out, "Keep your arses in or you'll lose 'em!" We get home and Aunt Louise calls us inta the house and Uncle John D. takes the bales of hay inta the barn. It's late September so the barn's fulla hay— hay we play in all the time—and between some of the rafters at the bottom we had strung up this binding twine that we used ta swing on. Well it happens that Uncle John takes the hay inta the top floor of the barn and it was dark and he musta tripped or sometin' 'cause he fell through one of the holes in the floor and went straight down to the bottom where he hung himself on the binding twine. Everybody was real upset. It seemed like such a weird way ta go. At the funeral everyone keeps whispering how morbid it was and Uncle John D. is lyin' in his coffin wearin' too much rouge and eye shadow and red lipstick and when Aunt Louise goes up ta kiss him all she can say is, "My God, he looks like a screamin' faggot, don't he?" I laugh a little and my Mum pinches me and tells me ta shut up. *(Pause.)* Then later on there was this big speech at the wake about how a person's last words are sometimes the most important and when my Mum asked me what the last thing Uncle John D. said I told her—"Keep your arses in or you'll lose 'em." She didn't believe me.

(Pause.)

CHLOE: I think Elvis just turned over in his grave. That story beats his by a mile.

ELLEN: It's the only one I've got aside from Zachary.

CHLOE: Did he really say that thing 'bout keepin' your arses in?

ELLEN: God's truth.

CHLOE: Wow. Maybe there's a hidden message in that.

ELLEN: I doubt it.

CHLOE: I mean they were his last words.

ELLEN: Doesn't mean anythin'.

CHLOE: What was the last thing Zachary said?

ELLEN: *(Quiet.)* He called me a stupid bitch.

CHLOE: What?

ELLEN: We were havin' a fight and he ended up callin' me a stupid bitch.

CHLOE: What were ya fightin' about?

ELLEN: I wanted ta adopt a baby. Zachary was against it.

CHLOE: Why?

ELLEN: I don't know. He loved kids. He always wanted kids. *(Pause.)* About a year after we were married I found out I couldn't have 'em. I couldn't have children so Zachary went out and bought fish. Miles and miles of fish, angelfish, goldfish, neonfish, Siamese fighting fish. You name it—he bought it. We musta had ten aquariums in the house—every single room except the bathroom—and every time I looked at them they'd remind me of how I couldn't have children and how Zachary wanted children more than he wanted ten aquariums fulla fish. And they knew that too, the fish knew that. So they'd laugh at me. They'd just swim around with their beady little eyes and laugh at me.

CHLOE: How do ya know they were laughin'?

ELLEN: They always bubbled whenever I came close ta them.

CHLOE: Maybe they were just tryin' ta say hello.

ELLEN: Hello my ass. They were laughing. And I hated them for it. For years I hated them. They made me hurt so bad inside that half the time

I felt like I just wanted ta explode. So when I finally decided I really wanted to adopt a baby I figured Zachary would be ecstatic. I figured we could finally get rid of all the fish and start a real family, but he said I was too old—that we were both too old—and even if we weren't, he didn't want somebody else's kid. And he didn't wanta get rid of the fish.

CHLOE: Is that when he called you what he called you?

ELLEN: No, that came later. We argued a bit and he went out ta the garage. I was so upset I started runnin' around the house tryin' ta think of some way ta get back at him. Then it came to me: I would get rid of those damn fish. All of them. So as soon as I was sure Zachary was still outside I started flushin' 'em down the toilet. I did it and I enjoyed it. I flushed a hundred and twenty-three fish. I woulda flushed more but the toilet clogged.

CHLOE: That's terrible.

ELLEN: I know. I couldn't find the plunger anywhere.

CHLOE: No, I mean the fish.

ELLEN: I wasn't thinkin' straight. I was so out of it I didn't even realize Zachary had come up the stairs until he called me a stupid bitch.

CHLOE: When he saw all those fish in the toilet he musta freaked.

ELLEN: He had a heart attack.

CHLOE: I'll bet.

ELLEN: No—I mean he really had a heart attack.

CHLOE: What?

ELLEN: That's when he had the heart attack.

CHLOE: And he died?

ELLEN: Right in front of me. There wasn't even a minute to call for help.

CHLOE: *(Quiet.)* Jesus. You killed him.

ELLEN: Please don't say that. That's probably what they're sayin' in the other room. Marybeth and Roy and all the rest. All of 'em blamin' me. I guess that's why I came out here.

CHLOE: I'm sorry—I didn't mean it like that.

ELLEN: I wanted a family so much and all I got was a dead husband and a bunch of dead fish. I keep repeatin' it over and over in my head and it still doesn't make any sense. I feel cheated.

CHLOE: I felt that way with Mom.

ELLEN: Cheated?

CHLOE: Yeah. And kinda guilty 'cause my bein' born made her die.

ELLEN: But that had nothin' to do with you. You couldn't prevent it.

CHLOE: It happened—and that's the way I always feel. Like you and Zachary.

ELLEN: I guess. I sure as hell didn't know he'd have a heart attack.

CHLOE: Now the fish are a different story. You are definitely a fish murderer.

ELLEN: Don't remind me. I'm depressed enough as it is.

CHLOE: Look on the bright side. *(Beat.)* At least they're in heaven with Zachary.

ELLEN: I wouldn't be surprised.

CHLOE: And Elvis is there too.

ELLEN: Elvis.

CHLOE: And Mom.

ELLEN: And Uncle John D.

CHLOE: And Einstein and Humphrey Bogart and Walt Disney and J.H.C.

ELLEN: J.H.C.?

CHLOE: Jesus H. Christ.

ELLEN: Him too.

CHLOE: Ya ever get the feelin' it's so lonely down here sometimes?

ELLEN: How do you mean?

CHLOE: Just that.

ELLEN: Sometimes. Yeah, I guess sometimes it is.

CHLOE: Makes ya kinda wonder if you're missin' out on somethin'.

ELLEN: Maybe.

CHLOE: I mean whatta ya think they do up there?

ELLEN: Sometin' tells me they watch over us, guide us.

CHLOE: You mean like right now?

ELLEN: Yeah, right now. Zachary's probably looking down wondering what the hell I been cryin' about. Probably still thinking I'm a stupid bitch but lovin' me just the same. He did love me. I know he loved me.

CHLOE: I had a dream about heaven once. It was like this great big game show with a zillion prizes. But it wasn't like an ordinary game show 'cause on this show everybody was a winner. Everybody. And no one ever actually got the prizes—they just kept gettin' the joy of winnin' them over and over again. And God—he looked just like Bob Barker.

ELLEN: Bob Barker?

CHLOE: Yeah. And when someone dies he'd just yell, "Come on down!"

(Pause. ELLEN thinks about it a bit and smiles. She thinks about it for another bit and lets out a small laugh. There are tears in her eyes and she wipes them and lets out another laugh—a laugh of recognition.)

(Confused.) What's so funny?

ELLEN: When I got up this morning I said ta myself, "This is gonna be one rotten day." And it was. All through the service I thought I was going to be sick—right there in the pew in front of everybody. I don't know what was worse—the thought of being sick all over my in-laws or the thought that for the first time in my life I was really truly alone.

CHLOE: *(Honest.)* I hate rotten days.

ELLEN: It was a real stinker, wasn't it? I never thought I'd get through it.

CHLOE: But ya did.

ELLEN: Yeah. I guess I did. *(Pause.)* Is my make-up running?

CHLOE: A little.

(ELLEN wipes her eyes with a tissue.)

ELLEN: Now?

CHLOE: It's better.

ELLEN: Good.

(She straightens her dress and then starts putting on her slightly shabby coat.)

CHLOE: Where ya goin'?

ELLEN: I don't know yet. I'm just goin'.

CHLOE: You won't tell anybody I was here.

ELLEN: No. I won't tell anybody.

CHLOE: Was nice meetin' ya.

ELLEN: It was nice meetin' you. Take care of yourself.

CHLOE: I will.

ELLEN: Bye Chloe.

CHLOE: Bye Ellen.

> *(ELLEN leaves either out the front door or up a flight of stairs. The lights begin to dim, leaving a spotlight on CHLOE. Pause. CHLOE glances upward.)*

Mom? If you're up there I hope you're watchin'.

> *(A single flower floats down from the sky behind her and the lights fade to black. The end.)*

Hindsight

by Dennis Foon

Characters

HE: A man.
SHE: A woman.

Setting

A park or any informal place where a person
might sit down to eat a bag lunch.

---

*(HE sits down at a bench, opens his briefcase, and takes out a
lunch bag. Before HE opens his bag, SHE enters and sits. SHE
opens her briefcase, takes out her lunch bag but does not open it.
Pause. HE starts to his open bag. SHE speaks, stopping him.)*

SHE: What is it today?

HE: I don't know, I haven't looked yet. *(Pause.)* I didn't make it.

   (Pause. SHE smiles.)

SHE: Who did?

HE: My wi—my roommate.

   (Pause. SHE smiles.)

28

Who made your lunch?

SHE: None of your fucking business.

> *(Pause.)*

HE: I'm sorry, I didn't meant to ... invade your privacy.

SHE: I'm sure.

HE: You work there, don't you. I've seen you.

SHE: I've seen you see me.

HE: You have?

SHE: With the little mirror.

HE: What are you talking about?

SHE: You know what I'm talking about.

HE: No.

SHE: In your pocket.

HE: Oh.

> *(HE reaches into his breast pocket and pulls out a small mirror.)*

SHE: That one. Why do you stare at me?

HE: I don't stare at you.

SHE: Through that mirror. I look up and see you in front of me, gawking.

HE: I don't. It's just—I have—I have an eye condition.

SHE: You spy on me through that little glass. You stare and imagine me naked. I can feel it, the pressure of that eye, pushing against me.

HE: I don't!

SHE: I'm at my desk and I feel the light glint, look up and see that bulging eye undressing me, invading me ... Aren't you eating your lunch?

HE: I'm not hungry.

SHE: Have a carrot.

HE: I'm sorry if it bothers you.

SHE: You're not sorry. It's an obsession.

HE: It's not, you see ...

SHE: It's a perversion.

HE: You don't understand—

SHE: It's an assault.

HE: It's not what you think, you see—I can't see out of this eye. It's totally blind. It's glass.

SHE: Glass?

HE: Glass.

SHE: Glass.

HE: I swear it. I swear it ... Would you like to see it?

(Pause.)

SHE: Yes.

HE: Right now?

SHE: Yes.

HE: Okay.

(HE takes out the eye and hands it to her. SHE examines it.)

SHE: Nice work. Local?

HE: No, Swedish.

SHE: Very impressive.

HE: You can tell? I found this amazing discount optical in Stockholm. Still cost a fortune but worth the price. No one knows glass like the Swedes. Must be all the ice. What do you think of the colour?

SHE: Beautiful. Intricate. It's a true hazel. My favorite. *(SHE swallows it.)* Skol.

(Pause.)

HE: You ate my eye.

SHE: I was hungry.

HE: I never looked at you through it. It was glass. I couldn't see out of it.

SHE: What difference does that make?

HE: All the difference.

SHE: It was still an eye looking at me. Like all the eyes that have ever looked at me, peered at me, pissed on me, scanned me with butcher's pupils. The only difference between this man's eyeball and all the other eyeballs is I ate this one.

HE: Give it back.

SHE: Too late.

HE: It's not, puke it out.

SHE: You want a puke-stained eye?

HE: I don't care. I need it.

SHE: Too bad. You stared. Your eye touched me. It became part of me.

HE: It was blind!

SHE: Irrelevant. You still used it, nearly free of guilt. But you knew it touched me. You knew it.

HE: I didn't. I swear.

SHE: You're lying.

HE: I was just checking it, for moisture.

SHE: You touched me, I touched you.

HE: But I didn't, I couldn't.

SHE: You did, you could.

HE: No I didn't, how could I? It was just an eye in a glass, it was nothing, just a reflection, a blind reflection! If a man can't do that, what can he do! *(Pause.)* It was just a small thing, such a minor act. Can't you see, it was an affection. For you. I just thought ... you might find some tiny part of me—of it—attractive. *(Pause.)* ... I thought ... if you noticed me looking ... you might reciprocate.

SHE: I did.

HE: You did.

(Pause.)

SHE: Thanks for lunch.

HE: You're welcome.

(SHE exits. HE opens his lunch bag. Looks in with his one good eye; closes it. The end.)

Nobody Waltzes Carrying a Thirty-pound Underwood

by Deborah O'Neil

Characters

BILLIE: A forty-five-year-old owner of a shop.
MARG: A forty-four-year-old customer.

Setting

A second-hand office equipment shop.

(MARG enters carrying a heavy old typewriter. She drops it on the counter.)

MARG: It's time we do some talking.

BILLIE: You got ten seconds of my undivided attention. What can I do you for?

MARG: You already did. I was in the other day.

BILLIE: Refresh my memory. Yesterday was one of those days. My mother could have walked through that door and I wouldn't have noticed.

MARG: And you would have screwed her too.

32

BILLIE: Billie Fishman sells only good stuff. He don't screw nobody.

MARG: That's "anybody." And I can believe it.

BILLIE: An expert in many fields no doubt. Look, Lady, and I'm being polite …

MARG: Ya. Well, I'm biting my tongue too.

> *(She turns the typewriter to face him.)*

> You sold me a broken down typewriter.

BILLIE: Well, we're all young once. The sign in the window says it all.

MARG: Pretend I can't read and listen up.

BILLIE: Everybody knows the odds.

MARG: And the customer is always right.

BILLIE: This is a second-hand shop. That means you're half right at best. You take your chances.

MARG: No, Mister, I don't take chances. I give them. And you got one.

BILLIE: You think you can just waltz in here and …

MARG: *(She laughs.)* You *are* the talker. Does it look like I'm waltzing? Nobody waltzes lugging a thirty-pound Underwood. This typewriter has major problems. And now you got me.

BILLIE: So, what'd you do to it?

MARG: Nothing. You're not listening.

BILLIE: You must have done something you shouldn't of. What do you do for a living?

MARG: I break boards with my bare hands. Wanna see?

BILLIE: It's all coming back to me now. Tattoos—lower right arm and left …

> *(He motions to his chest area.)*

MARG: Breast. It's called a breast.

BILLIE: Charlie, Tripper, Spank. Spank? You wanted to build up your speed and I can only imagine what the hell that means.

MARG: Ya, well, that was yesterday when I thought I was getting a good deal. When I thought I could buy a half-decent typewriter from an a-okay shop. Today I'm just the tattooed typist who wants to break boards real fast with her bare hands.

BILLIE: I bet you square up all your problems that way.

MARG: No. Sometimes I like to break them real slow.

BILLIE: Pushing decent people around.

MARG: Well, I wouldn't have a problem if there weren't decent folk like yourself screwing me around.

BILLIE: And if you take it out on people, what's to stop you from giving the typewriter a few good whacks if it doesn't first do what you want.

MARG: Well, who would have guessed I'd meet Dr. Freud in a second-hand office equipment store.

BILLIE: The name's Fishman.

MARG: I remember. Billie. Right? You told me yesterday when you slid your greasy palm across my twenty bucks. Billie with an "i," "e." Almost sounds like family. Well, Billie, this typewriter doesn't do what you promised it would.

BILLIE: Let me look at your hands.

MARG: Again? *(As if she doesn't hear the command.)*

BILLIE: Your fingers. Let's have a look.

MARG: Nobody touches these hands unless I give the say so.

BILLIE: Come on. Come on. Lift them up.

(She lifts them up to him.)

What do you know, no brass knuckles but then who would have thought …

(She lowers her hands from view.)

Don't look much like typing fingers to me, either.

MARG: That's probably because there is no typewriter.

BILLIE: You're not a gentle person by nature are you?

MARG: This is a piece of equipment.

BILLIE: Everything in this world's got to be respected.

MARG: Look who's talking about respect.

BILLIE: Especially precision equipment.

MARG: And I'm telling you this machine got the best of my attention. I coaxed it, I stroked it, I soothed it, I massaged the ribbon. I did everything except take this typewriter to bed with me.

BILLIE: Each to his own.

MARG: Nobody got more respect than this machine.

BILLIE: You didn't read the manual, then.

MARG: I read the manual. Inside out and upside down trying to make head or tail.

BILLIE: And where was the typewriter all this time you were relaxing and reading? Eh? Probably still in its case by the front door.

MARG: Do you see a case? There is no case.

BILLIE: That's what happens when you go for the cheap. You can't buy a decent typewriter for twenty bucks these days. I don't know what you were thinking. Twenty bucks don't even fill up a gas tank.

MARG: You talked me into it. You told me this was the best buy for my money.

BILLIE: So what's your beef?

MARG: The beef is, I trusted you.

BILLIE: I mean with the typewriter. What's wrong with the typewriter?

MARG: It doesn't like my words.

BILLIE: *(He laughs.)* And I do? So, what didn't it like?

MARG: Lots.

BILLIE: Let's just hear one.

MARG: The words are beside the point.

BILLIE: No, the words are the point.

MARG: The point is honesty.

BILLIE: You come in here saying the machine don't type words. I want to know the words. Name one. Bet you can't.

MARG: If you'd stop talking for a minute I could think.

BILLIE: Gladly. I got to see this.

MARG: *(Correcting.)* Have to see this.

BILLIE: Whatever. *(He watches her think. Pause.)* Well?

MARG: "Ladies." It wouldn't type "ladies." There's one. A simple salutation—

BILLIE: Ladies are never simple.

MARG: Dear ladies.

BILLIE: *(Stands over typewriter.)* What'd it like better, broads?

MARG: *(At him.)* There's only one way to spell the word, "ladies," Einstein.

BILLIE: Well, there are ladies and then there are ladies. If you're not even sure, how do you expect a machine to figure it out.

MARG: And you'd know all about that. The King of Junk, locked up here in some stuffy old store all day. You probably still live with Mama.

(He gets uncomfortable, tries to move the typewriter out of the way. She stops him.) And does your Mother know that you screw ladies for a living?

BILLIE: You're not my idea of a lady.

MARG: Does she know you rip people off all day? Or did you forget to tell her you weren't president of the Chamber of Commerce.

BILLIE: I never sold you nothing that you didn't want to buy.

MARG: No, you just forget to tell me that it hasn't worked for ten years. You thought I wanted to type in some language I can't even read. *(She waits. No answer.)* Don't you ever get twinges around your heart when you take advantage of people?

BILLIE: And you should talk. Coming in here like gang busters. Threatening me with physical violence.

MARG: You wouldn't know anything about being physical with a woman, would you Billie? You've been living your life with beat-up old typewriters too long.

BILLIE: I know a lady when I see one, don't you worry.

MARG: Just like you know a fast buck?

(He opens the cash register.)

BILLIE: Here, you want your money?

(He slams the money down on the table. She gives the twenty-dollar bill back.)

MARG: I didn't come in here to get my money back.

BILLIE: Take it. You're lucky I'm in a giving mood.

(He pushes the twenty back to her.)

MARG: That would be too easy. *(She gives the twenty back to him.)* No, I'm going to give you lots of time to think about what you did to me.

BILLIE: I'm going to forget the sign outside.

MARG: *(She laughs again.)* Screw the sign.

BILLIE: What, you want blood? Okay. Hit me. Get it out of your system. That's the way you work, isn't it?

MARG: Don't try to analyze me. Better people than you have tried.

BILLIE: Isn't that your M.O.? And I'll even bet those names tattooed all over your body are the poor slobs you K.O.'d.

MARG: Don't point your finger at me. You've got more of a past to worry about than I do.

BILLIE: Somebody disagrees with you, slug it out? Some man looks at you the wrong way, you want to go ten rounds.

MARG: You're damn right because I was stupid enough to trust them, too.

BILLIE: Well, Billie Fishman don't make apologies for nobody but himself.

MARG: And I came here to get a typewriter and I'm not leaving without one.

   (Pause)

BILLIE: Okay, I'll exchange it. That's the best I can do. I'll give you another model.

MARG: I want this one.

BILLIE: What is this? First you don't like it. Now you like it. Make up your mind. What do you want from me?

MARG: I want you to fix it or whatever needs to be done.

BILLIE: This ain't no repair shop. You're really something, Lady. You can't just waltz in here …

MARG: I told you I don't waltz.

BILLIE: You waltzed in here like you owned the joint. I saw it with my own eyes.

MARG: Saw what?

BILLIE: Well, your back.

MARG: And what about my back?

BILLIE: It's just that it was poker straight and the way you hold your head high, like that. It makes the rest of you just fall in underneath. Kind of like a pendulum.

MARG: *(She laughs.)* A pendulum? And what are you trying to sell me now? Some broken down clock? 'Cause I don't need any more of your … precision equipment.

BILLIE: No, I mean it. I can almost hear the tick-tock standing right here. Listen.

MARG: You're such a bullshitter. I'm not even moving.

(Pause)

BILLIE: You're smiling.

MARG: That's not a smile. That's a smirk. You get them when you have to lug heavy typewriters all over hell's half-acre.

BILLIE: No, no. I know smirks. I know sneers and grins, too. You don't think I know a smile when I see one?

MARG: Suit yourself.

BILLIE: What's the last thing that made you smile? Besides one of my typewriters.

MARG: None of your damn business.

BILLIE: When's the last time you talked to your plants? *(She laughs.)* There's another one. *(Points at her smile.)*

MARG: So who says I got plants? You have been cooped up too long. Next thing you'll be asking me to talk to that typewriter. Like it has a personality. Feelings or something.

BILLIE: And why not? You got to learn to talk. Open yourself up.

MARG: Talk is cheap. Look at you.

BILLIE: Talk is my business. Where would I be if I couldn't talk you into buying from me?

MARG: I'd have a typewriter that works.

BILLIE: And I'd be over forty, out of business and living with Mom.

MARG: And talking to your geraniums.

BILLIE: It works. You got to try it.

MARG: I did, once. I felt plain stupid.

BILLIE: Keep trying. It gets easier.

(Pause.)

MARG: I do have this ivy.

BILLIE: Nobody keeps ivies any more.

MARG: Well, you asked me and I told you. What'd you think I kept— the Venus Fly Trap.

BILLIE: I just never figured you for an ivy-leaguer.

MARG: Well, it's not like I got a whole garden or something. I got one, in the kitchen window. But it's doing okay.

BILLIE: And what about you?

MARG: Let's keep it to second-hand typewriters and leave me out of it.

BILLIE: Okay, I'll see what I can do. With the typewriter, that is.

(He turns the typewriter towards himself.)

I'll need your name and number? So I can call you when it's ready.

MARG: It's Diner. Marg Diner. It's really Margaret but nobody's calls me that anymore. Just Marg.

BILLIE: *(He types, repeating her name.)* Marg with a hard "g."

MARG: Diner.

BILLIE: Diner.

MARG: And that's one "n" in Diner.

BILLIE: I know that but the typewriter has ideas of its own. You're going to have to settle for Dinner.

MARG: Dinner I can live with. It's the apology I'm waiting for.

(The end.)

Escape from Golf Camp

by Rebecca Shaw and Andrew Wreggitt

Characters

LIZ: A middle-aged woman wearing the latest in pastel polyester designer golf wear. Good-looking golf swing.

LARRY: A middle-aged, hard-working guy. He has a terrible golf swing, but is good-natured and eager to learn.

JACK: A very fit and muscular golf instructor. He has a helmet of thick blond hair and a brace of flashing white teeth. The Jimmy Swaggart of golf.

Setting

The practice tee at a very posh golf camp.

(LARRY and LIZ are at the practice tee, hitting imaginary golf balls towards the audience. They both look a little weary. LARRY hits a ball. LIZ leaps back out of the way as it shanks almost straight to the right.)

LARRY: Sorry.

LIZ: *(Looking where the ball went.)* I can't believe you hit the little truck again.

LARRY: I know. That's eleven times this morning. *(Calls out.)* Sorry about that.

> *(Just then JACK enters. LARRY and LIZ see him and immediately go back to their practicing.)*

JACK: I believe I hear talking going on somewhere on this practice tee. What I want to hear are the sweet little voices of those tiny golf balls going "snick, snick." If we want to ascend to the heavenly regions of the single digit handicap we must … *(He leans very close to LIZ.)* What is it we must do, Elizabeth?

LIZ: *(Reciting.)* We must concentrate …

JACK: *(A joyous shout.)* Concentrate! Yes! Onnn …?

LIZ: On our legs and hips …

JACK: *(Puts a hand on LIZ's hip.)* Because …?

LIZ: Because we have to let our body do the work …

LARRY: *(Joins in enthusiastically.)* … instead of our arms!

JACK: Yes! *(Puts his arms around LIZ from behind and guides her through a swing, ignoring LARRY.)* I feel the digits dropping from your handicap as we speak. Keep up the good work! *(Pulls away from her and turns to LARRY.)* As for you, Lawrence, I would appreciate it if you would try to avoid hitting my ball-collecting truck. You've only been here three days and the driver is developing a nervous twitch. *(A flourish of his hand.)* Back to work!

LARRY: *(Timidly.)* Do you think we could take just a short break, Jack?

LIZ: We could use a rest.

JACK: *(Pauses, then sweetly.)* Rest? You'd like to rest? Oh, certainly! Resting is very natural. Why just look at the thousands, nay millions, of golfers who have never broken a hundred. All very well rested, no doubt. All those thirty-six handicappers with their duck hooks and their banana-ball slices, their knock-kneed stances and baseball grips, all topping their tee-shots and sculling their irons. But very well rested.

LARRY: Okay. You're right.

LIZ: We'll keep going, Jack.

JACK: *(Hand to his ear.)* Listen! Do you hear that?

> *(They listen.)*

Those are the agonized cries of millions of duffers blowing one chip shot after another! All because they lack the fundamentals of a good basic golf swing! *(Nearly sheds a bitter tear.)* The needy are so many and I can share my gift with only so few. *(Turns and smiles again.)* But if you'd rather rest than practice ...

LARRY and LIZ: *(Both swinging vigorously.)* No, no ... really.

JACK: Good.

(JACK stalks off while LARRY and LIZ keep swinging, looking furtively over their shoulders.)

LARRY: You know, my friends warned me that going to golf camp would ruin my game.

(They both watch one of LARRY's drives start out left, then slice wildly to the right.)

Actually, it's gotten better.

LIZ: One guy told me that taking lessons upped his handicap by ten strokes. Took him six months to get his game back to where it had been before.

LARRY: They're just jealous.

LIZ: Absolutely.

LARRY: Who wouldn't be, eh? Five glorious days of golf camp. Nine holes before breakfast, long irons in the morning, chipping and putting in the afternoon, a quick eighteen holes before bed. I mean we get to sleep right on the golf course! The bed-spreads are even green.

LIZ: The inspirational tapes under the pillow ...

LARRY: *(Quoting.)* "Jack Nicklaus on St. Andrew's, 1974, drives a four-iron 325 yards from tee to green and drops his putt for an eagle!"

LIZ: I heard that one last night, too!

LARRY: All this for just two thousand dollars ...

LIZ: ... a day. It's incredible, isn't it?

LARRY: A chance to bring our best concentration to the game without outside distractions.

LARRY and LIZ: Golf is so much more a mental...

LARRY: ... game than a ...

LIZ: ... physical one.

(They both get momentarily embarrassed by their enthusiasm and lack of discretion.)

We better not let Jack catch us talking.

(LARRY and LIZ go back to swinging. LARRY hesitates, then:)

LARRY: Your name is Elizabeth?

LIZ: Liz. And you're …?

LARRY: Larry.

LIZ: "Twenty-eight handicap. Wants to play the senior tour when he turns fifty."

LARRY: *(Smiles and points at her.)* The newsletter. You're Liz, the twelve from Winnipeg. *(Quotes.)* "Rainbows in the fresh morning dew, the spray of a well-stroked putt on a wet green." I thought your poem was beautiful!

LIZ: *(Blushing.)* Thank-you.

LARRY: No. I mean it. It was … inspiring.

(LARRY takes another swing. They both watch it arc from left to right again.)

LARRY: Hey, look out … fore!

(They both wince.)

LIZ: It's uncanny. Even if you were trying to do it on purpose you couldn't hit him …

LARRY: … twelve times in one morning. I know.

(They go back to swinging again. JACK reappears and walks up to LIZ. He has a camcorder and is filming her swing.)

JACK: Good, good.

LIZ: Why do I suddenly feel like I'm on national television?

JACK: Don't be nervous. You know, Elizabeth, I think we should have a private tutorial later tonight. I think it's time to introduce a slight fade to your drive.

LIZ: Wow! That'd be great!

JACK: Check the Future Missionaries of Golf bulletin board for your time.

LARRY: What about me, Jack?

JACK: Lay off my truck, okay, Lawrence.

(JACK leaves.)

LIZ: Isn't he great?

LARRY: *(Looks a little down.)* Yeah, great.

LIZ: *(Notices.)* Oh, don't be discouraged, Larry. Give it time.

LARRY: It's no use. I was born with a slice. I must have come out of the womb left to right. I can't even ride a bicycle straight. It's like a genetic flaw, or some kind of character defect.

LIZ: You're being too hard on yourself.

LARRY: That's just it. I'm starting to realize that I love the perpetual failure, too. I love everything about this game. *(Self-conscious.)* You must think I'm crazy.

LIZ: No, I don't. I feel the same way.

LARRY: I love playing the sundown rate on the public courses ...

LIZ: And trying to finish the eighteenth in the dark.

LARRY: Poring through the golf magazines, studying the pro tips ...

LIZ: Ordering those useless devices that are supposed to improve your game for only $14.95 plus shipping and handling ...

LARRY: Getting three sets of knitted head covers with tassels for Christmas ...

LIZ: Wearing pastel polyester slacks ...

LARRY: *(Getting more breathless.)* The feel of golf tees in your pocket ...

LIZ: Getting drenched while you're putting by a pop-up sprinkler ...

LARRY: And then when you get that ...

LIZ: Yes ...

LARRY: That one-in-a-million ...

LIZ: Yes, Larry ...

LARRY: Perfect ...

LIZ: Shot!

LARRY: *(Following an imaginary shot.)* Snick!

LIZ: It's a game of endless possibility.

LARRY: Failure and redemption.

LIZ: Ecstasy and agony.

> *(They stop and look at each other. She blurts out.)*
> Larry? Are you married?

LARRY: Not anymore. My wife didn't understand golf. She thought I was crazy because I wanted to move to the Yukon where ...

LIZ: ... you can play golf twenty-two hours a day in the summer. I know! It's my dream, too!

LARRY: And you? Are you married, Liz?

LIZ: *(Shakes her head, becoming emotional.)* No. Not anymore. But I owe him so much. He taught me to play golf.

LARRY: Did he ... die?

LIZ: *(Shakes her head.)* I became a twelve handicap. He stayed a thirty-six. It was too much for him. He got the Saab. I got the Ben Hogan woods.

LARRY: *(Looking into her eyes.)* Liz?

LIZ: Larry?

(JACK reappears and sees them looking dreamily at each other.)

JACK: You've been talking.

(They turn and resume their positions, guiltily. LIZ swings.)

Elizabeth, you need to move the ball more into the middle of your stance. Let me show you what I mean. *(He sets up to hit a ball.)* When I hit a ball the way you were standing ...

(JACK hits the ball. All three of them watch a perfect tee shot that goes on forever. LARRY's eyes nearly fall out watching it.)

JACK: That wasn't as bad as I meant it to be.

LIZ: That's one of the best drives I've ever seen.

JACK: Let me try it again.

(JACK hits another gorgeous drive. LIZ and LARRY just stare.)

JACK: My apologies. It's hard to demonstrate bad habits when you've been blessed with a near-perfect golf swing.

LARRY: *(Hitches up his belt, swaggers a little.)* Here. You better let me do that.

(LARRY swings. They all watch the ball go straight to the right.)

JACK: Not the truck again!

LIZ: *(Grimaces.)* Ugh. He had the window open. Must have thought he was safe over there.

JACK: *(Calls over.)* Somebody call an ambulance. *(To LARRY.)* Larry, I want you to take this head cover and hold it between your knees. *(LARRY does it.)* Now try to touch your left nipple with your chin ... and slowly draw the club back as far as you can. Turn your belt buckle toward your target.

(LARRY struggles to achieve this, grimacing. There is a pause.)

LARRY: Now what?

JACK: Now, Larry, I want you to ponder your own golf worthiness. This is what the end of your golf swing looks like: a knotted rope, a tangle of fishing lures, a coupling of amorous orangutans, midget wrestling! Although they say there are many paths to the Golf Head, there may not be one for you. Larry, it's like we're all trying to get to say … the north pole. Some of us start in Baffin Island, some in Toronto, some in Miami. But you, Lawrence … you are deep in the frozen wastes of Antarctica at the bottom of a glacier. They say that back in geological time the north and south pole were once reversed. And given enough time, providing the sun doesn't nova, they may yet be returned to their former positions and your handicap may drop from a twenty-eight to a twenty-five. *But I doubt it!*

LIZ: Just a darn minute! Where do you get off talking to him like that?

(LARRY starts to untangle himself.)

JACK: My dear, I once coached Lee Trevino.

LIZ: And he's never been the same. *(Becoming passionate.)* Oh sure, you know how to golf, Jack, but so what? Do you love the game the way this man does? I don't think so!

LARRY: *(Taking heart.)* Yeah.

LIZ: So what if he plays out of a lot of sand traps.

LARRY: That's what they're there for.

LIZ: You're not a real golfer, Jack. You're just a hairpiece with good extension on your back swing.

JACK: Oh, yeah?

LARRY: Yeah!

JACK: Well, if that's the way you feel, why don't you just leave?

LIZ: Maybe we will.

JACK: Oh no, you won't. You can't leave. You're addicted. You're sick. What will you do without your instructional videos, your free practice ball machine? You'll never leave!

LARRY: Yes, I will. I may be a golfo … a golfo …

LIZ: C'mon Larry, say it!

LARRY: A golfoholic. Yes! My name is Larry and I'm a golfoholic! But that doesn't mean I can't control my own life.

JACK: Hah! Then walk away, Larry. Walk away from golf camp! Just remember, you're a twenty-eight handicap. Ha, ha, ha, ha, ha.

(JACK leaves.)

LIZ: We can do it, Larry! I'll go with you! We can start again, we can learn to live with our handicaps, we can be happy. I know we can!

LARRY: Oh, Liz!

LIZ: Larry!

LARRY: Let's go! Wait! How will we get out of here? They picked us up at the airport, we're miles from anywhere …

(They both look over at the truck.)

LIZ: The truck. They loaded the driver into an ambulance. We'll take his truck.

LARRY: And it's full of …

LARRY and LIZ: Golf balls!

(They're about to leave when LARRY stops.)

LARRY: Do you think we could just …

LIZ: Hit one more for the road?

(They look at each other, then quickly line up. They swing in unison, then stare off straight ahead. Their mouths drop open.)

LIZ: Oh my God!

LARRY: Did you see that?

LARRY and LIZ: The perfect shot!!!

(They look at each other, then reach down for another ball.)

LARRY and LIZ: One more!

(The end.)

The Two of Us

by Doug Melnyk

Characters

A WOMAN and a MAN.

Setting

A room with a television.

WOMAN: I can see the two of us, sitting up, drinking coffee, sitting on the giant overstuffed couch, staring with blank relief at the television. It's the early stage of a weekday evening. It's like I'm overhead, somehow. I can see the couch, centered in the middle of a large, dark room, television in the lighted half, all brightness and light, and behind us, behind our big couch, darkness, darkness of the winter night, the uncurtained windows, and the heavy darkness of the room itself. Persian carpets and dark pieces of unloved furniture, gifts from the outskirts of the city, the suburbs.

MAN: And I can see her, out of the corner of my eye. And when I close both eyes, I can imagine her more fully. The dark flush on her forehead, as she gets more sleepy. Her full lips relax, just a bit.

WOMAN: I can see him, snoring for a bit, until finally—one big snort—he wakes himself up. Looking at me, so sheepish. His face looking slack.

MAN: I can see her smiling fondly at me, with the kind of fondness that only comes with time.

WOMAN: He's the model, he's the one they talk about, the King of Cable. He's watching his past, present and future flying past his face on fifty-seven channels. He's watching his mother's hopes, his father's source of shame, playing on alternate channels—the shopping channel, the religious network, the sports channel, the French channel—he's mesmerized by nothing in particular and everything in general, a general awareness of limitless possibilities, of sympathetic scenes, of dreamy situation ... No, he's just mesmerized by the rhythm. He doesn't want to pick anything. Flying films, and advertising projects, somebody's expensive nightmare, somebody's million-dollar baby, flying by his face like numbers on a Roll-a-dex, flapping across his relaxed baby face like the colourful plastic brushes flapping across the car windows at an automatic car wash. He doesn't want to pick anything. Not just yet.

MAN: I ask her if she'd like to settle down on one program, so I stop to consider this adventure program. It's not a big budget film. Would she want to settle on this one, do you think?

WOMAN: So what the hell is this? Six stupid teenage guys carrying a tombstone—it's dark out—carrying a big, white tombstone across a deserted intersection, and running into the lane, each one of them skulking there.

MAN: As she sits there, staring idly at the screen, I can tell by the candid way her features respond to each channel ... that here, at home, with me and only me, does she feel completely ... at home—does she feel completely ... herself.

WOMAN: This one guy, middle-aged it looks like, is being interviewed about his teenage years of mischief: "Yeah, yeah, we stole tombstones. Well, I, well we, were young, hell, and strong! We were baseball players, for God's sake! You'd get this thing home and man, that wasn't easy, six big guys in excellent physical condition carrying a tombstone down the street, on a rainy night, for six city blocks! But, when you got the thing at home, it was the most perfect, the most excellent coffee table. It was so shiny and beautiful, so easy to wipe off. The only thing was, you couldn't put anything hot on top of it. It got all covered with burn marks from all of our coffee cups."

MAN: Did you know that people still stop and stare at you when you walk down the street? You haven't lost it, you know.

(WOMAN sneezes, three times, one after the other, before compos-ing the features of her face again. By this point, MAN's attention has inevitably returned to the television set.)

WOMAN: Look at him now, fiddling with his hair again. He does have a god-given gift of hair. Even I admit it. He can make his hair look like—different people—like, see? He can get his hair to look a little bit like Geraldo. And now, sort of like JFK, sort of, sort of, like Phil Donahue, like, Sharon Carstairs in the old days, like, Albert Einstein, like Carol Channing. Oh, please, stop it. Stop it already.

(MAN slowly stops fiddling with his hair and then sneezes, loudly, three times in a row.)

I don't know. When I first met him, he didn't even own a television set. He liked to cook.

MAN: Try our new salad bar, just loaded with crisp and sparkling garden delights.

WOMAN: He would embarrass me with compliments. I was embar-rassed by the way he looked at me in public. Honestly! Well, in those days when we did go out.

MAN: Just go ahead and dig in. Go ahead and savor that just-picked freshness.

WOMAN: I remember our first date. He cooked me dinner at his apart-ment. You wouldn't believe it. It was a fantastic apartment. We went driving after dinner. It was early in May. You know what it's like then? A clear sky with no moon. Driving outside the city, driving past one small town after another, the sky just seemed to become more and more clear.

MAN: Remember Carl Sagan's program, Cosmos? Remember the se-ductive way that he talked about the infinity of the universe. So many nights now, when it gets warm enough to finally stare up at the stars, I get that old feeling again, and it reminds of the first time that I saw that program, Cosmos.

WOMAN: I'll never forget that night.

MAN: Billions and billions …

WOMAN: I had never met anybody else quite like him. The way his mind worked, the way his mind could leap like a gymnast.

MAN: Billions …

WOMAN: I had been around a lot, I had travelled all through Europe. So what was it about him?

MAN: Oh, and I saw this show the other night, about "Back from the Dead" stories. It seems like, for some people, Heaven and Hell are right here on this earth, and then, that it's just all up to you, yourself, to make it all happen.

WOMAN: But, what I really remember the most about travelling are all the hassles, the lineups, the customs people, language problems. I guess it's just my attitude, just my perspective.

MAN: Sometimes, these people would have, maybe an accident on the operating room table, for instance, and then, they would see their own bodies, as if from a great height. And then, they might go on some kind of … journey.

WOMAN: Nowadays, I'm happy to stay close to home. It's all here, isn't it?

MAN: Their stories were all so similar. Does it really seem like a coincidence to you?

WOMAN: I'm older now, I don't have the patience for an eighteen-hour flight anywhere. Does that limit my options?

MAN: They show one guy go zooming through this long tunnel with a lot of bright lights at the other end, and all these close-ups of people who were supposed to be his friends when he was a kid. Then, you know, the warm and overpowering feeling of love from some power bigger and better than the rest of us.

WOMAN: I've been sick often enough on the plane. I thought that I would get over it. And I didn't.

MAN: The feeling of warmth, that should encompass all humanity, and then some—they used to call it "brotherhood."

WOMAN: A hotel room is not a home. I need my man, I'll admit it.

MAN: The sound of bells, they showed a million tiny Christmas lights all wrapped in gauze, the whole production was very well supported, it wasn't really a modest film at all. But, anyway, bells, the lights, the feeling of being at one with all who have gone before and also with those who will go after, and also, let me remember, the feeling of arrival! The end to pain and sorrow! Yes!

WOMAN: Maybe it would have made a difference to stay at a really good hotel, to really have a ... treat.

MAN: And some scientists say that death is completely technical, and that everything will eventually be re-worked and re-designed.

WOMAN: Also, I miss my cat. My treat is to stare directly into the watery eyes of my old cat, just forget about myself, and nod off, on this fat, ugly couch. I just stare into her eyes, and my brain just goes ... idle.

MAN: Some scientists say that there's a neuro-transmitter in the brain. And when you die, or almost die, it can sort of short out. And this bright light that everybody talks about—when they tell their back-from-the-dead stories on early-morning talk shows—is just like the light that you used to be able to see, on your television screen, after you turn it off. You turned the machine off, and the sound disappeared quickly, like a whimper, but the picture was distilled into a tiny white glowing point, that lingered and lingered, sometimes for fifteen or twenty minutes.

WOMAN: Completely at home, completely myself. See me, as if from a great height? On the couch with him, and this cat, and the waterfall of images which move consistently, bounced as a message from the remote control at his wrist, the rhythm moving directly from his pulse, from a major artery. We're waiting for something.

MAN: Some of this stuff is honestly better than university. Who could argue? I saw this one program, about the different ways that men and women have of watching television. This one expert, he talked about this idea of the hunter-gatherers. He said that all the women traditionally gather food, that they know all about the edible plants in a certain area. You know, that they would like to settle on one program, and watch the whole thing from start to finish. But, the men, this program said, the men have to follow the herds. See the guy on the couch, with only enough energy—or so you'd think—to keep endlessly searching and searching through those fifty-seven channels. Is he that different from his distant relative, the ancient hunter? They're both prepared— sometimes by training but always by instinct—to know just what to watch for. To put an end to everyone's unbearable waiting, and then, like their noble ancestors, to finally take action.

(The end.)

Out of Body

by Beverley Cooper

Characters

MIRANDA and GILLIAN.

Setting

The food-court at a mall.

(MIRANDA sits at a table with a tray of bad Chinese food in front of her, trying to separate a pair of cheap chopsticks. She is still bundled in her coat. MIRANDA is meek, mild and, seemingly, afraid of life. She spots another woman, GILLIAN, across the room and waves her over. GILLIAN has a tray of food—a healthy looking salad.)

GILLIAN: You're eating all that for lunch? Isn't there MSG in that?

MIRANDA: Oh … I don't know. I—

GILLIAN: Did you know those chopsticks are made from trees that are cut down in the rain forests of Brazil? … Also known as the shrivelling lungs of the world.

MIRANDA: They are?

GILLIAN: Aren't you hot?

53

MIRANDA: A little, but it just seems like a bother to get—

GILLIAN: How's Tom?

MIRANDA: He's fine. You know. Same old Tom.

GILLIAN: You know I'd never meddle but I can't see that he's right for you.

MIRANDA: Tom? What makes you say that?

GILLIAN: You're so different.

MIRANDA: You hardly know him. Do you?

GILLIAN: Well enough. You get your hair cut or something?

MIRANDA: No, does it look it?

GILLIAN: Maybe you should, y'know, try a change.

MIRANDA: Oh dear.

GILLIAN: Was there something you wanted to talk to me about? I'm afraid I've only got a half an hour.

MIRANDA: I don't know where to begin. Well I guess I should start by saying that … I suspect that I am *(Whispers.)* going crazy … either that or—

GILLIAN: What?

MIRANDA: Crazy … my head's not quite right. No, that's not true. My head is fine but the things that are going on out of it are not fine. I mean I feel alright but strange things have been happening. Oh, I'm all mixed up.

GILLIAN: I've got the perfect therapist. I'll get you hooked up with him. He's done wonder for me, let me tell you … looks just like Gregory Peck. He deals with—

MIRANDA: I don't think that would be quite right. Maybe I should start at the beginning and you see what you make of it.

GILLIAN: Why didn't you say there was a beginning, sounds juicy.

MIRANDA: A couple of months ago I was in bed and began feeling these … vibrations.

GILLIAN: Miranda, is this going to be sordid? I'll start taking notes.

MIRANDA: Gillian … please … let me continue. It's very difficult.

GILLIAN: Whoops. Sorry. Vibrations.

MIRANDA: Yes, vibrations … sort of an electrical surge … throughout my body … several nights in a row … I couldn't sleep. Well this one night I was tossing and turning and my hand was dangling over the side of the bed, my fingers touching the floor. I stretched my arm a little and I realized my hand was reaching right through the floor. I pushed a little harder ... I felt the wood, the sawdust, a bent nail. Suddenly I realized what I was doing and pulled my hand out. I was terrified.

GILLIAN: Sounds like a bad dream to me.

MIRANDA: That's what I thought too! But I couldn't stand not knowing. So, in the middle of the night, I went downstairs got a saw and cut a hole in the floor to see what was there.

GILLIAN: You cut a hole in the floor?

MIRANDA: It was exactly as I felt: the thickness of the wood, the pile of sawdust, the way the nail was bent!

GILLIAN: Maybe it was a vision! You know some people have visions about the future ... you have visions about floorboards.

MIRANDA: That was only the beginning. A few nights later, I was having my usual difficulties sleeping, the strange vibrations ... I was worrying about the new filing system at the library, about Brian Mulroney and about Tom—

GILLIAN: Tom?

MIRANDA: He'd been distant as of late. And I just thought it would be nice to be able to fly away, get away from it all. Well the next thing I know I feel my back against a ... hard surface ... like the floor ...

GILLIAN: Another floorboard vision.

MIRANDA: I felt around ... it didn't feel right ... the moon was shining through the window ... casting a soft glow over the bed ... as my eyes got used to the light I realized that ... Gillian ... I was floating.

GILLIAN: How floating?

MIRANDA: I could see my body in bed, sleeping. But my mind and another part of my body was floating on the ceiling.

GILLIAN: It must have been an acid flashback.

MIRANDA: But I never touched acid. Not any drugs! Ever.

GILLIAN: Maybe you should have. Miranda, I think you need something more than therapy. Freudian analysis. Stress management. At the very least a colon flush.

MIRANDA: That's just it! I've been checked over by my doctor. He says I'm the most healthy and sane patient he's ever had.

GILLIAN: Doctors! What do they know?

MIRANDA: But it's so real. I float every night. I go places and see things. Slowly at first, because I was frightened. But then I started to feel more in control. I could will myself to go out the window. The first time I just peeked and then darted back into my body. And then I went a little farther, over to the house next door, looked in the third floor window ... the little boy was reading a book with a flashlight. I didn't wish to scare him ... I even thought it might be illegal, looking in other people's windows so ... I tried not to do it anymore. However I couldn't stop myself from floating ... It felt so liberating ...

GILLIAN: Have you talked to Tom about this?

MIRANDA: No ... he seems so preoccupied in his work and it never seemed like the right time.

GILLIAN: Is there more?

MIRANDA: Yes! One time I got a little too bold. I went too far too soon and I got lost. It was awful. I kept thinking about my poor soul being separated from my body forever ... Everything looked different. My eyes were seeing things as if from a new perspective—sort of a blurry mass of senses. Panic took over. I darted hither and thither to find my house but to no avail. Then I felt another presence beside me. Pushing my elbow, guiding me back to my body. I was so relieved ... not only to find my house again...but that I wasn't alone ... there were others that could float too.

GILLIAN: We'll get you a spot on Oprah. She can interview a collection of floating librarians.

MIRANDA: I will not have you make fun of me. I don't want to hear any librarian jokes.

GILLIAN: I heard one just the other day. How many librarians does it take to change a light bulb?

MIRANDA: *(Resigned.)* How many?

GILLIAN: Shhhhh!

MIRANDA: That's not even remotely funny. I should have known better than to confide in you.

GILLIAN: What do you expect me to say? You float. It's beyond my comprehension. I don't happen to know any other floaters. It's weird. You need help. People don't float.

MIRANDA: I thought you were open minded. I thought you were my friend.

GILLIAN: I've got to get back to work. Why don't we talk later?

MIRANDA: I have proof.

GILLIAN: Proof of what?

MIRANDA: About my experiences.

GILLIAN: What … you saw E.T.?

MIRANDA: Tell me, Gillian … what were you up to last night?

GILLIAN: Pardon me?

MIRANDA: At about ten o'clock. What were you doing?

GILLIAN: At ten o'clock? I was at home.

MIRANDA: Doing what?

GILLIAN: In bed, reading a book.

MIRANDA: No you weren't.

GILLIAN: What is this—the Spanish Inquisition? Are you going to pry those chopsticks under my fingernails?

MIRANDA: I don't need to. I know exactly what you were doing at ten o'clock the night of *[Place the previous day's date here.]*

GILLIAN: *(Getting her coat on.)* This is insane. You're insane. The fluorescent lights have affected your brain patterns. I'll meet you after work and then I'll drag you to the nearest loony bin.

MIRANDA: You were with Tom.

GILLIAN: What?

MIRANDA: You were with Tom. I saw the whole thing. Cuddling up, watching pornographic movies, with my boyfriend. I was just going to peer in your window, see what you were wearing … to give myself proof.

GILLIAN: And what was I wearing?

MIRANDA: One of those cheap nighties you bought at the lingerie party that Sabrina MacMillan had.

> *(Pause.)*

GILLIAN: And what was the movie?

MIRANDA: Last Tango in Paris.

GILLIAN: I'd hardly call that pornographic.

MIRANDA: Dirty. Filthy. With my boyfriend! My best friend! My ex-boyfriend. My ex-best friend. *(She looks at her watch.)* I've got to go.

GILLIAN: What can I say?

MIRANDA: Just tell me I'm right.

GILLIAN: *(Pause.)* You're right.

MIRANDA: Good. Now tell me I'm not crazy.

GILLIAN: *(Pause.)* You're not crazy.

MIRANDA: Tell Tom his dirty laundry will be in a plastic bag by the garbage cans.

GILLIAN: Wait. Can't we talk this over?

MIRANDA: I've got my first meeting of believers—of out-of-body experiences—people like me ... I've got a whole new life ahead of me and unfortunately it doesn't include you, Gillian. By the way— Tom prefers his socks ironed.

GILLIAN: I'll see you around!

MIRANDA: No you won't see me ... but I might see you.

(MIRANDA exits. After a moment GILLIAN picks at MIRANDA's Chinese food, and eats her leftovers. The end.)

Louis and Dave

by Norm Foster

Characters

LOUIS and DAVE are in their early twenties.

Setting

Dave's car. Two chairs, side-by-side, make up the set.

(LOUIS and DAVE are cruising a downtown city street. DAVE is driving. When they are yelling at women, their speeches may overlap.)

LOUIS: Hey sweetheart! Hey! You in the pants!

DAVE: Hey! Hey gorgeous!

LOUIS: You wanna go for a ride? Huh? Whadya say? Go for a little ride?

DAVE: Hey! We're goin' to a party. You wanna come? Come on, climb in!

LOUIS: Come on! Hey! I think I love you! I'm in love! Marry me! Whadya say?

DAVE: How about your friend there? She wanna go to a party? Whadya say, baby? Huh? *Party!!*

LOUIS: I love you!

DAVE: *Party!*

LOUIS: I mean that!!

DAVE: *Party!*

LOUIS: I want you!!

    (Pause.)

DAVE: Are they lookin'?

LOUIS: No.

DAVE: Snobs.

LOUIS: Stuck up is what they are.

DAVE: Icebergs.

LOUIS: A couple of glaciers.

DAVE: Damn right.

LOUIS: They weren't even good lookin'. Did you think they were good
    lookin'?

DAVE: I've seen better.

LOUIS: Damn right.

DAVE: Much better.

LOUIS: Absolutely. It's a good thing they didn't come over.

DAVE: Whew! Are you kiddin'? Can you imagine bein' stuck with
    those two?

LOUIS: Tell me about it.

DAVE: Gimme a break.

LOUIS: *(Pause.)* So, what do you think, Dave, the Flames gonna do it
    this year or what?

DAVE: Definitely.

LOUIS: You think so?

DAVE: No question. They've got it together this year. They've got the
    coaching, the scoring punch, they're okay in the nets. They'll be there.

LOUIS: I think you're right, man. I really do. The only ones who can
    give 'em a run are the Bruins. Maybe the Rangers. *(Pause.)* The
    Kings too maybe.

DAVE: Hey, don't count them out.

LOUIS: They're tough. They're tough.

DAVE: *(Pause.)* And you got the Habs too.

LOUIS: Yeah, they're always there at the end. Could be, could be. Oh, here come three more. Slow down, slow down. Hey, sweetheart! Hey! Hey, honey! You wanna go for a ride?

DAVE: Hey, beautiful! Your prayers have been answered baby, we're here! Hey!

LOUIS: Hey, nice sweater. Did it come with those bumps or did you pay extra for those? Huh? Hey!

DAVE: Hey, you in the red! You're killin' me! You're knockin' me out!

LOUIS: Come on, come back! Hey!

DAVE: Where ya goin'?

LOUIS: Come over here!

DAVE: Where ya goin'?

LOUIS: You don't know what you're missing girls!

DAVE: Where's the fire?

LOUIS: Guys like us don't just fall out of trees you know.

DAVE: Damn right. You'll be sorry.

LOUIS: Bye-bye!!

DAVE: Bye!

LOUIS: Bye-Bye!! *(Pause.)* I don't think they heard us.

DAVE: I don't think so.

LOUIS: Too bad. They were gorgeous too.

DAVE: They were hot, Louis. Hot.

LOUIS: They were major hot.

DAVE: I think I saw steam.

LOUIS: God, I love Saturday nights.

DAVE: They're the best.

LOUIS: How long we been doin' this now, Dave?

DAVE: Gee, I don't know. Three, four years.

LOUIS: Like clockwork, right?

DAVE: Every Saturday.

LOUIS: Damn right. And one of these nights we're gonna score.

DAVE: No doubt about it.

LOUIS: Damn right.

DAVE: Gotta happen.

LOUIS: We're due.

DAVE: Absolutely.

LOUIS: You got it.

DAVE: Absolutely.

LOUIS: *(Pause.)* Hey, the Jeff Healy Band's in town next Thursday. You wanna go?

DAVE: Jeff Healy?

LOUIS: Yeah.

DAVE: They're gonna be in town?

LOUIS: Next Thursday.

DAVE: All right! You're not kiddin' me are you?

LOUIS: No way.

DAVE: All right! Dig it.

LOUIS: So, you wanna go??

DAVE: Definitely.

LOUIS: All right!

DAVE: Oh, wait a minute. I can't next Thursday.

LOUIS: Why not?

DAVE: My reading club meets every Thursday.

LOUIS: Your what?

DAVE: My reading club. Damn. Talk about bad luck.

LOUIS: What reading club? What the hell is that?

DAVE: It's a reading club. We meet every Thursday and read books.

LOUIS: Books?

DAVE: Yeah.

LOUIS: You read books?

DAVE: Yeah.

LOUIS: What kind of books?

DAVE: All kinds. Everything from Hemingway to Plato to Camus.

LOUIS: To what?

DAVE: Camus.

LOUIS: What, you mean that killer whale thing?

DAVE: No, that's Shamu. Camus was a French writer. An existentialist.

LOUIS: Oh.

DAVE: Oh, babe alert! Check out those hard bodies. Hey, gorgeous! Hey! You and your friend wanna go for a ride?

LOUIS: Hey, sweetness! What's your name? Will you marry me? Huh? Please?

DAVE: Whadya say? You need a lift? Where you goin'? Hey, don't go away.

LOUIS: Come on over, I'll give you a tour of the back seat here. It's nice and bouncy! Like you!

DAVE: No, they're gone.

LOUIS: I thought they were gonna come over there for a second.

DAVE: They looked this way I think.

LOUIS: Yeah, they did.

DAVE: They were lookin' at the car behind us actually, but it was in our direction.

LOUIS: Absolutely. *(Pause.)* So, you don't wanna go see Jeff Healy, huh?

DAVE: I'd love to, man, but the group is counting on me.

LOUIS: Hey, no problem. *(Pause.)* Wanna get together and watch some football tomorrow?

DAVE: Uh … No, I can't. Geez, the Niners are playin' tomorrow too, aren't they?

LOUIS: Niners and the Bears. A classic.

DAVE: Oh, man. What a day for the symphony to be in town.

LOUIS: The what?

DAVE: The symphony. They're giving a concert tomorrow afternoon and I've got tickets.

LOUIS: The symphony?

DAVE: Yeah. I mean, I'd skip it, but it's Mahler.

LOUIS: Smaller than what?

DAVE: No, not smaller. Mahler. The composer. And done the way Mahler should be done, well, it can be very moving.

(He spots some more women.)

Oh, here we go. Look at this. Four of them! And dressed to kill. Hey, honey!! Hey! You girls wanna go for a spin?? Whadya say? One of you will have to sit on my knee! Huh? What do you think? It don't bother me if it don't bother you! Hey! Hey, guess what! My friend here isn't wearing any underwear! Hey! *(To DAVE.)* Gee, that usually gets a rise out of them. Oh, well. Their loss.

LOUIS: Very moving?

DAVE: What?

LOUIS: What the hell is that? Very moving?

DAVE: What, Mahler?

LOUIS: Yeah. Since when do you go to the symphony?

DAVE: I always go. Whenever they're in town.

LOUIS: You never told me this.

DAVE: No?

LOUIS: No.

DAVE: Are you sure?

LOUIS: I woulda remembered.

DAVE: Well, I don't know. I guess it never came up.

LOUIS: The symphony.

DAVE: Yeah.

LOUIS: With all those instruments and girls holding violins between their legs?

DAVE: Cellos, yeah. You wanna go sometime?

LOUIS: I'm sorry?

DAVE: They'll be in town again soon. You wanna go?

LOUIS: Lemme get back to you.

DAVE: Sure. *(Pause.)* Little slow tonight, don't you think?

LOUIS: Little bit.

DAVE: Man, you wanna talk about nice babes, I was at this "Women for a Better Future" rally last night, and you shoulda seen some of that action. Ouch! I'm talkin' mega-hot.

LOUIS: Women for a what?

DAVE: Women for a Better Future. It's an organization that's trying to bring the plight of today's single mother to the government's attention. You know, trying to get them better allowances, trying to make daycare more accessible to them. Things like that.

LOUIS: And what were you doing there?

DAVE: Well, I sympathize with these women. They've got a heavy burden to bear.

(Yelling at a woman on the street)

Hey, sweet cakes! Are you lookin' for a few good men? Well, here we are, honey!!

LOUIS: Dave ...

DAVE: And we are bein' all that we can be, Ladies, and wait 'til you see how much that is!!

LOUIS: Dave?

DAVE: What?

LOUIS: Do you ever get the feeling that ...

DAVE: That what?

LOUIS: Well, that maybe we're drifting apart?

DAVE: What? No. You and me?

LOUIS: Yeah.

DAVE: Are you kidding? No chance.

LOUIS: You don't think so?

DAVE: No way. Drifting apart. What makes you say that?

LOUIS: I don't know.

DAVE: Drifting apart?

LOUIS: It's just a feeling I got.

DAVE: Come on. How long we known each other?

LOUIS: Eight years.

DAVE: Since grade ten, right?

LOUIS: Right.

DAVE: Drifting apart. Get serious. We're like two peas in a pod. We're like brothers. We're practically mirror images of each other. Geez. You know, Camus has a theory about a mirrored image universe ...

LOUIS: Dave, Dave, Dave ...

DAVE: What?

LOUIS. Not now, huh?

DAVE: Sure. I guess you're right. There's a time and place for Camus. You know what I think it is, Louis. I think maybe you're a little miffed because I can't go to the Jeff Healy show with you and I can't come over and watch football. Is that it?

LOUIS: Naw ...

DAVE: Huh?

LOUIS: Naw ...

DAVE: That's it, isn't it?

LOUIS: Not really.

DAVE: Louis?

LOUIS: No, it's ... all right, maybe that's got something to do with it, but ...

DAVE: I thought so. Well, listen, let me make it up to you.

LOUIS: Whadya mean make it up to me?

DAVE: I wanna make it up to you.

LOUIS: How?

DAVE: Well, the National Ballet's performing at the concert hall in two weeks. Why don't you be my guest?

LOUIS: What?

DAVE: You won't have pay a cent.

LOUIS: You go to the ballet too?

DAVE: No, I'm in it.

LOUIS: What?!!

DAVE: Well, I'm not one of the principal dancers or anything. I'm just in the chorus.

LOUIS: Pull over.

DAVE: What?

LOUIS: Pull over.

DAVE: What's the matter?

LOUIS: Nothing, just pull over. Right here.

DAVE: *(Pulling over.)* What's the problem, Louis? You gonna ralph?

LOUIS: No, I'm going home.

DAVE: What?

LOUIS: I'm going home.

DAVE: Home? What for?

LOUIS: How long have you been with the ballet?

DAVE: I don't know. 'Bout two years.

LOUIS: Two years. And you didn't even tell me?

DAVE: What's to tell? We're nothing special. We pull our tights on one leg at a time like any other ballet company.

LOUIS: I gotta go.

(He gets out of his seat and stands.)

DAVE: But, we were just getting hot, Louis. You don't wanna hit on the babes anymore?

LOUIS: No, I've lost the mood.

DAVE: Just for another half hour.

LOUIS: No …

DAVE: Twenty minutes. I'm feelin' lucky.

LOUIS: No, I gotta go. Really.

DAVE: Oh. Well, at least let me drive you home.

LOUIS: No. No, I'd rather walk.

DAVE: What's the matter?

LOUIS: Nothing. I've just … I've got a lot to think about.

DAVE: Boy, you're really steamed about this football thing, huh? Well, listen, if it's that important to you I'll skip the Mahler.

LOUIS: No.

DAVE: No, I mean it.

LOUIS: No …

DAVE: It's only Mahler, what the hell. I mean, it's not like it's Brahms or Mozart.

LOUIS: Dave, no. You … you go to the Mahler. I don't care. The thing is, man, I don't understand why you never told me any of this before.

DAVE: I did tell you.

LOUIS: No, you didn't. Never. You've never told me none of this stuff about symphonies or books or tights. Nothin'

DAVE: *(Pause.)* You're right, Louis. I haven't.

LOUIS: Well, why?

DAVE: Well … I guess I figured that if you found all this out about me. You wouldn't want to hang with me anymore.

LOUIS: What?

DAVE: Yeah, you know, me bein' an intellectual and all. I thought that might turn you off. But, then … well, I couldn't hold it in anymore. I mean, it was tearin' me up. Tryin' to hide all this, it was like I was livin' two lives. That's why I let it spill tonight. I just wanted to get it out in the open, you know?

LOUIS: So, you're an intellectual?

DAVE: Yeah.

LOUIS: Oh, man.

DAVE: I know.

LOUIS: I knew you wouldn't like it, Louis. But, hey, that's okay. I mean, at least it's out there now and we don't have to pretend anymore. And if you don't wanna hang out anymore, that's okay too. I understand.

LOUIS: I feel used, Dave.

DAVE: I know.

LOUIS: I feel cheap.

DAVE: I know.

LOUIS: *(Pause.)* You're not interested in politics too, are you?

(DAVE says nothing. He nods his head in shame.)

Oh, man. Not that too. You mean like you know all about this GST stuff and about what a New Democrat is??

DAVE: Yeah.

LOUIS: Oh, man. You shoulda told me, Dave. You shoulda told me a long time ago. Maybe I coulda gotten used to the idea, but to spring it on me now, man …

DAVE: I know. I was wrong. I'm sorry.

LOUIS: Well, you should be. I trusted you. And you misused that trust.

DAVE: I'm sick about it, Louis.

LOUIS: I guess.

DAVE: Just sick about it.

LOUIS: Geez.

DAVE: *(Pause.)* Well, I guess I'll get goin'.

LOUIS: Yeah.

DAVE: You're sure you don't want a ride, huh?

LOUIS: No. I ... I just wanna be alone right now.

DAVE: Okay. *(DAVE puts the car in gear.)* Don't hate me, Louis. I mean, I hope we can part as friends. *(LOUIS doesn't answer.)* No. I guess not. We'll see you, Louis.

LOUIS: *(He turns to walk away then turns back.)* Hey, Dave?

DAVE: Yeah?

LOUIS: Same time next Saturday?

DAVE: *(Pause.)* Damn right.

   (LOUIS watches him drive off, then walks away. The end.)

Confinement

by Rachel Wyatt

Characters

JANET, sixty-nine years old, and KRISTY, her daughter.

Setting

The stage is bare.

(JANET is sitting in a wheelchair facing the audience.)

JANET: *(With difficulty.)* A-a-a-b-b-b-c-c-cow. B-r-o-w-n c-o-w. *(She wheels her wheelchair round in a full circle to face the audience again and begins to speak confidentially.)* Her friend Bar-bar-a called. Bar-bar-a! I wouldn't be talking to you like this but I have to talk to someone.

(Pause.)

She's the world's great volunteer, my daughter Kristy. She'll help anyone. Except me. What does it matter if a man takes to wearing turquoise? That's his problem. It's a hard colour anyway. It only suits very young blondes—of either sex. He's fifty-three if a day. Started to wear turquoise and this Bar-bar-a, goes crazy, calls Kristy. Cries on the phone and Kristy goes running over there. Running! Poor

Bar-bar-a. Got to help. Leaves me here on my own. No one to talk to except you.

(Pause.)

And just look at my hair. When I began teaching, I had a dress, turquoise, and everyone complimented me on it. I was blonde then. Young. And the dress fitted where it touched as my mother used to say. I went to dances. I was very popular. And Kristy's father lifted me off my feet when we twirled around. Right off my feet. Right off my feet. Right out of my mind! So we got married. And then she was born. *(She grimaces with remembered pain.)* And he never lifted me off my feet again. Died ten years ago. Left us alone. Me and her. Died ten years ago. Left us alone. Her with her post office job and me now retired. And it's Saturday, and she's supposed to ... I'm not complaining but she has let me down. It's always the last person who calls who gets her attention. And what her excuse was this time was that her friend Bar-bar-a was in floods of tears because her husband had gone out in a turquoise sweater she had never seen before. And he was wearing a shirt to match underneath. *(Leans forward.)* And this is a tragedy!! She tells me all this, does Kristy. They've told her to talk to me. I heard them telling her to talk to me more. And what I'm asking myself this last hour and will go on asking—I'm asking you now—is, is that—a man going out in an unaccustomed sweater—a good reason for me being left here without my errands done or my hair washed? Well is it? "I'll come back later," she said. "As soon as I can," she said. Having clean hair matters to me. I brought her up to help others. I can see that wasn't necessarily a good thing. But it's hard now for me suddenly to say, "I come first." It goes against all I taught in the classroom, at home. Help others, be kind to others, I've always said. And this is what happens. She is kind—to others. I shan't let her see I'm upset. *(Hearing a noise, she turns.)* Is that her? K-k-k ... No one there. I can wash my own hair. I'm not a burden. Not helpless. She likes to do things for me. It makes her feel good. "Today I washed my mother's hair." I washed hers often enough. If you work it out from zero to twelve when she began to wash her own, I'd say I washed hers about twice a week, fifty-two times two times twelve. One thousand, two hundred and forty-eight times. It seemed like more. And at least I don't wriggle and scream except when she gets the water too hot. *(She listens for a moment and then continues.)* She was difficult from the beginning. I never let on. She may have, may've heard me once or twice telling the neighbours or a friend, over coffee—you know those conversations. It's what you talk about sometimes, isn't it. Three days I was in labour. Of course you mention it now and then. I mean it's one of the events of your life. What else has such significance as the birth of a child? *(She looks round cautiously. Whispers.)* Is she back already? *(There is no sound. She talks normally again.)* Kristy, I've said to her once or twice, maybe more times, you're very precious to me. You came within that of costing me my life. I never did quite get over it. If the doctors said it was a miracle once, they said it twenty times. But that's not responsible, she, her birth, those three days of torture, for me being like this now. Confined again! Ha. Though the doctor did say when I pressed him that strokes can be caused by trauma that happened early in life. I wouldn't want her to think that. I can bear this. I'm learning to move again. *(Wiggles a hand and fingers.)* A-a-a-a-b-b-b-b-A brown cow dances every Friday. I wasn't a teacher for nothing. I've heard Kristy say "My mother's a very determined woman." She says it with pride. She's a good daughter and I have no regrets. She was worth every moment of that dreadful, searing pain. Every single moment. *(She recalls the birth and grimaces.)* You love them all the more, don't you, the difficult ones. Those three days left me with a problem inside which I'm not about to describe in detail except to say that there are parts of me twisted in there in such a way that doctors wonder how I function. How did I function? They shake their heads. But I have a fine daughter. And she'll know all about it one day—maybe. She's thirty-eight and she goes running off to help every woman who cries out. She's thirty-eight and not getting any better looking. I'm her child, she said the other day to me. *(She stops to listen but there's no one there.)* If she had a child, how would we manage? She said that. She asked. How could we manage! I laughed. I would hold it, sing to it, tell it stories. Baby-sit every day. But she would have to suffer the pain herself. I told her that. You have to be honest about these things.

(Pause.)

When I can walk again, when I'm all right, I'm going to go away. I've got friends that keep asking and asking me to stay with them. I'm not dependent. No one can say I'm spoiling my daughter's life. I want her to have a chance, to go through what I went through so she'll understand.

(She hears KRISTY coming and slumps down in her chair. KRISTY enters and comes to the wheelchair behind her mother)

KRISTY: *(Briskly.)* Hello Mother. How are you? I wasn't very long, was I? Barbara sends her love. She was feeling a lot better when I left.

JANET: A-a-a-b-b-b-

KRISTY: Come on then. Shampoo and rinse. I'll try not to get soap in your eyes this time—or water down your back.

(KRISTY begins to push the wheelchair out.)

JANET: A-a-a-b-b-b-c-c-c-cow. T-t-t-turk. Cow.

KRISTY: Very good, mother. Two whole words. We'll have you talking again in no time.

(Exit. The end.)

Beverly Hills Waiting for Godot

by Elise Moore

Characters

X: A teenage girl about sixteen or seventeen years of age.
O: X's best friend, same age.
TEACHER: Female.

Setting

Two teenage girls are trying to hold a conversation to combat the boredom of yet another high school assembly. They're sitting in the gym, which can be represented by a bench. The girls are to be played by male actors. They should be dressed in minimalist drag—just enough to "suggest" that they're teenage girls, and not screaming drag queens.

(As the scene begins, the two girls, and the TEACHER off to one side, are standing as the sound of youthful voices singing O Canada dies away. The girls look suitably bored and disrespectful and collapse on the bench the second the song ends.)

X: That sucked.

O: The choir queers are sounding especially anemic this year.

(They stare ahead listlessly for a few moments.)

74

Did she say it's a pleasure to be undressing us?

X: Addressing, dear. Kim brought alcohol. Little wee tiny bottles. She stole them while she was baby-sitting.

O: Smells like teen spirits.

X: Do your song.

O: What song?

X: Your Nirvana song.

O: It's Nir-vaw-na, not Nir-va-na, like Madonna, not banana. *(Sings.)* Nir-vaw-na, Nirvana, Madonna, banana, let's call the whole thing— fucked!

X: *(Pretentiously.)* Personally, I don't think it's Nir-vaw-na at all. I think the trendy-bitches just pronounce it that way to sound all intellectual-bohemian.

O: They're wanna-bohemians.

X: *(Looks around.)* Go back to your Portable Zen Readers, you existential zeroes. *(Pause.)* Do the song. The Hepatitis song.

O: Not now.

X: Come on. I'll start. *(Sings under her breath.)* Oh no, oh no, oh no, oh no …

O: *(Sings.)* In yer anus—hepatitis! It's contagious—don't remind us! It's a sickness, and a virus, In yer anus—hepatitis!

> *(They start laughing loudly, stopping only when the TEACHER walks past them, glaring disapprovingly. They're silent for a few moments, staring straight ahead.)*

X: When is this going to end?

> *(Pause.)*

O: Who do you think is the sexiest cartoon duck?

X: What?

O: Ducks, cartoon ducks! Which is sexiest? Daffy, Donald, Duckula or Darkwing?

X: Oh Darkwing, definitely.

O: I've always been kinda partial to Daffy. All in black, like a trendy-alternative. I bet he listens to Ministry. Or Morrissey. *(Pause.)* What're you doing after this?

X: Yer mom.

O: *(Pointing at the audience.)* Oh look, look—they're going to introduce the football players.

X: *(Mock excitement.)* Christ in a blender!

O: We can figure out which ones are ... *(She holds out her arm and lets her wrist hang limply.)*

X: *(Claps her hands.)* Oh, goody! I'm in the mood to out the whole world.

O: Me too. Ever since I figured out about Bugs Bunny.

X: What about Bugs?

O: That he's ... *(Does the limp wrist action.)*

X: *(Incredulous.)* No way.

O: Way way!

X: Not Bugs. Bugs can't be ... *(Wrist action.)*

O: "What's up, Doc?" The carrot?

X: *(Realizing the awful truth.)* Oh my God.

O: And then he always dresses up as a girl-bunny and marries Elmer Fudd? *(World-wearily.)* Get off the island, Gilligan. And what about Puff?

X: Who?

O: Puff the Magic Dragon.

X: Shut up.

O: Drag-on?

X: I mean it.

O: "Frolics in the autumn mist"? How many heterosexual mythical creatures do you know who frolic?

X: *(Puts her hands over her ears.)* I can't hear you—

O: *(Getting louder.)* Lives by the sea? We're talking major-league saltwater here, sweetheart. And hangs around in caves, with little boys?

X: *(Shouting.)* Don't pollute Puff!

(The TEACHER returns and leans over them, glaring.)

TEACHER: *(In a stage-whisper.)* Do you think you ladies could keep it down, please?

(The TEACHER walks away. The girls stare in silence.)

X: What time is it?

O: I can't see the clock.

X: *(Pointing.)* Ooo, look at that one.

> *(X and O look at each other, then quietly sing to the tune of Monty Python's Lumberjack Song.)*

X and O: I'm a macho-jock and I'm okay, I sleep with men but I'm not gay … *(Pause.)*

X: I have to take a wicked piss.

> *(She suddenly starts to clap, at first energetically, then, seeing O's lack of enthusiasm, her clapping peters down and finally stops.)*

That sucked.

O: What're you doing after this?

X: I don't know. Nothing.

O: Want to come over?

X: Okay.

O: And eat a whole bunch?

X: Okay.

O: And then throw it all up?

X: Okay. *(Pause.)* What should we eat?

O: Yer mom. *(Pause.)* I don't know. Nachos.

X: Uh-uh. They burn. Jalapenos, you know.

O: Ice cream.

X: Yummy!

O: Tastes just as good coming up as it does going down. *(Pause.)* When're you seeing Gene next?

X: *(Suddenly dreamy-eyed.)* Tomorrow night. We're going to nookie. Me and my Sweet Baboo. My honey-booger. My—*(She notices O's disgusted look.)* What's wrong? What? I'm sorry. What?

O: You're talking like a Care Bear again.

X: I'm sorry.

O: Here he comes.

X: Here who comes? Not another … *(Does wrist action again.)*

O: No. It's the president. The black president of the whitest school under the ozone layer. Just look around at all the WASPs. White Anglo-Saxon Perverts. All radiating Politically-Correct-er-Than-Thou-ness. After all, it's not trendy to be prejudiced. And trendiness is next to godliness. But I'm prejudiced. I'll admit it. I'm hyper-prejudiced against all races. None more than my own, of course.

X: I like our president. He's an okay guy. Not a snob. Doesn't snub. Always says "hi" in the halls. And gives me noogies. *(Frowns.)* I hate noogies.

O: He's too socially conscious and environmentally friendly. *(Scornfully.)* I bet he still has all his brain cells.

X: *(Mock outrage.)* Screaming Jesus in a centrifuge! He ought to be shot.

O: *(Delivering a sermon.)* I'll tell you what's behind the hallowed halls and hollow heads of our high school. The 3-Ds of the Blank Generation: We're decadent, dysfunctional and de-sensitized.

X: What are you talking about?

O: My degeneration.

X: You make it sound so complicated.

O: This is the story of Generation X, not the story of 90210. *(Suddenly, viciously.)* I don't care about the environment!

X: You're in your own little world in any event. Here comes the cheer.

O: I detest cheap sentiment.

X: *(Now deliberately rhyming.)* It must mean the end is near.

O: *(Joining in.)* There's definitely something apocalyptic in the air.

TEACHER: *(Shouting letters in response to an imaginary figure.)* C! A! L! V! I! N!

   (At the same time, X and O shout out their own version.)

X and O: Y! E! R! M! O! M!

TEACHER: Calvin!

X and O: *(Simultaneously, with the TEACHER.)* Yer mom!

   (The TEACHER beams and claps. O mocks enthusiasm, jumping up and down, cheering and clapping loudly. X watches her, giggling. O sits back down, bored and listless as before.)

X: *(Consoling her.)* I think it's almost over.

O: What's the point? We'll just find some reason to get bored again.

X: I like being bored. Boredom motivates me.

O: To do what?

X: To find happiness.

O: *(Catching on.)* Do you have happiness inside you?

X: No, but I will tomorrow night.

O: Do you have happiness in the palm of your hand?

X: No, but I will—

O: *(Interrupting.)* What're you doing?

X: Making puns to pass the time.

O: I mean after this.

X: *(Looks around.)* It isn't over yet?

O: *(Looks around.)* I'm not sure. I don't think so. How am I supposed to know if you don't?

X: I don't know.

O: Well, I'm going out for a smoke.

X: Now?

O: When it's over.

X: Oh. *(Pause.)* All I've got is gross rollies today. They look like baby joints.

O: Little wee tiny joints. *(Pause.)* Kim brought booze.

X: I know. *(Pause.)* What kind?

O: I don't know. *(Pause.)* This is all getting too hypothetical for me.

> *(O takes out a cigarette and puts it in her mouth.)*

X: *(Claps her hands with glee.)* It's a Heathers moment.

O: I'm not going to light it.

X: *(Disappointed.)* Oh.

> *(The TEACHER approaches them once more.)*

TEACHER: *(In a stage-whisper.)* Do you think you could wait until you get outside to take out the cigarette? We have some visitors with us today, and it doesn't look very good for the school image.

O: *(Sweetly.)* Sorry.

> *(She puts it away and the TEACHER walks away. Furious.)*

Whore.

X: *(Sympathetically.)* I know.

O: Whore whore whore whore whore whore hairy old whore. *(Mimicking nastily.)* "It won't look good for the school image." This may not be the school "image," baby, but this is the school. We're the school, us and the fags and the druggies and all the rest of the freaks. Not the jocks or the trendies or the pseudo-bohemians or the self-styled outcasts—

X: Or the skaters.

O: Or the skaters.

X: Or the hackeysackers.

O: Or the hackeysackers. *(Holds her head in her hands and moans in an extravagant show of teenage angst.)* Where am I? What's happening? I don't understand!

X: What don't you understand?

O: Hackeysackers!

X: Hackeysakers are the extra sensual heroes.

O: *(Correcting her.)* That's existential.

X: *(Sweetly.)* No.

(Pause.)

O: I need a cigarette. Which, by the way, has nothing to do with finding hackeysackers extra sensual.

X: Oh, you know you do.

O: Shut up.

X: Kiss my hackeysack, baby. *(Pause.)* Too bad I didn't take out one of my rollies. Then she'd really've freaked. "It doesn't look very good for you to be smoking pot during assembly."

O: I'm having a nicfit.

X: I'm having a flashback.

O: Can we go yet?

X: I think so. Everyone else is gone.

O: *(Looks around.)* Are you sure?

X: *(Looks around.)* Seems pretty empty to me.

O: Nobody's here?

X: Just us.

O: Everyone's ... elsewhere?

X: Excluding the obvious.

(Pause.)

Should we go find them?

O: No. Let's stay here.

(The end.)

(Handwritten notes in top margin:)

Flashlight
cookee
bandaid

whale music

Bic
Cigarettes
Camera

Whale Watch

by Colleen Curran

Characters

TED: A newspaper photographer.
MAURA: An environmental activist.

Setting

Inside the stomach of a whale.

(Handwritten, circled: unplug)

(Darkness. The sounds of the ocean, then of whale song. Lights come up to reveal what appears to be a cave with ribs. It is half filled with water and two people, a woman and a man, are bobbing in small outboard motorboats side by side. It is pitch dark and they cannot see each other.)

MAURA: *(Calling.)* Hellllllllooooooo? Is anybody in here with me?

(She searches through her army pants pockets.)

Ohhhh, I hope I brought it. I did. I did.

(She pulls out a flashlight.)

Please let it work.

(It does. She uses it to get a better view of her surroundings until it illuminates the man in the next boat.)

⌈plug in⌉

Ohh. Hi. Have you been there the whole time?

TED: Yes.

MAURA: Why didn't you say anything?

TED: I recognized your voice.

MAURA: You did?

TED: And I thought: all this and her, too.

MAURA: How come you know my voice?

TED: Because it carries so much over your bullhorn. I was also at your rally.

MAURA: *(Smiles.)* Yeah? You were?

TED: By assignment, not association.

(He shows her his camera case.)

MAURA: Did you get any good pictures?

TED: It doesn't matter now.

MAURA: Yes it does. You must have gotten some great stuff.

TED: My last one was of the bull whale opening his mouth.

MAURA: That'll win you a few awards.

TED: If I can beam it out by satellite. We are not getting out of this one.

MAURA: We are so. Lots of people know where we are.

TED: So will the rest of the world pretty soon.

MAURA: Yes. So somebody will rescue us pretty soon.

TED: How are they going to find us?

MAURA: There aren't that many sperm whales left in the world. He'll have to surface for air.

TED: Then what? Is somebody from Sea World gonna coax him into giving us up peacefully?

MAURA: Maybe. If they found the Titanic, they can find us.

TED: That only took seventy-three years. And it stayed in one place.

MAURA: They've probably called out the navy. The subs. Scuba divers.

TED: I'm sure they'll want to conduct a million-dollar search and rescue for a woman whose friends spend their free weekends dodging harpoons and sabotaging ships. They'd love to save a bunch of rich, old hippies whose hobby is Environmental Terrorism.

MAURA: Who are you calling terrorists? What about those butchers out there? They don't care that these animals are protected by international agreements. They don't care about quotas or size limits or extinction. All they care about is harvesting the most incredible creatures on this planet for fertilizer and cosmetics and animal feed!

TED: Save it, sweetheart. I heard it all back on shore.

MAURA: How can you not care?

TED: The only thing I care about is the fact that I am someplace nobody will ever find me. I'm not in a landslide or a cave-in or lost in space even.

MAURA: They will find us. *(Smiles.)* Pinocchio found Gepetto.

TED: Pinocchio?

MAURA: Somebody will find us. Stop complaining and being so sarcastic. We're lucky we're still alive and in one piece.

TED: Oh we're real lucky. Moby Dick spared us this time.

MAURA: Don't drag Moby Dick into this. He's the cause of whale hate and distrust in the world. They're friendly mammals.

TED: Our guy was super friendly. He tried to eat the whaling ship.

MAURA: After it attacked his friends.

TED: Then he swallowed us. And probably broke my finger.

MAURA: It's bleeding.

TED: A bit.

MAURA: *(She takes a small first aid kit from her pants.)* Let me fix it.

TED: What's the point?

MAURA: Don't get pessimistic with me. You've got more reason to get out of this than I do.

TED: Why's that?

MAURA: *(She bandages his hand.)* Think of the photo opportunities in here. You'll get a National Geographic cover out of this.

TED: How can you be so up? So cheery?

MAURA: I'm not going to let myself get depressed about this.

TED: How do you plan to manage that? Large doses of Seconal?

MAURA: I look on the bright side. I did what I set out to do. What happened to me probably stopped the whale hunt. And the one we're inside of, got away. *(Pause.)* I think your finger might be broken.

TED: So what? How long is your flashlight good for?

MAURA: Hours. It has those last and last batteries.

>*(TED takes out a package of cigarettes.)*

TED: Want one?

MAURA: *No!* And neither do you.

TED: Don't start telling me they're bad for my health.

MAURA: They're bad for his.

>*(SHE points to whale.)*

TED: I'd have to smoke sixteen cartons a day for three years.

MAURA: This isn't a bus or an airplane or an elevator. This is a living organism.

TED: So is this.

>*(TED takes out his Bic lighter, lights it and MAURA flicks the cigarette out of his mouth into the water. He stares at her, calmly takes out another cigarette, and this time MAURA tosses the entire package in the water.)*

That was deliberate. The first time could have been a mistake.

MAURA: It wasn't.

TED: You animal rights activists make me sick. What about human rights? You Greenpeacers and Save the Whales and Sea Shepherds, you're all nuts. Fanatics. Maniacs. Know what I did to one of your kind last winter? A big blizzard and one of your Greenpeaceniks is at my door canvassing to Save the Seals. Know what I did? I slammed the door in his face. That's what I did!

MAURA: Are you finished?

TED: *No!* When we get out of here, I'm going to sue you.

MAURA: I'm glad my act inspired hope.

TED: Do sperm whales beach themselves?

MAURA: They'd need a very large beach.

TED: My luck this type doesn't go in for mass suicide. Come on, please, be the exception.

MAURA: Then it would die.

TED: But we'd have a chance of getting out alive.

MAURA: At what cost?

TED: At what cost! I'm right. You *are* crazy.

MAURA: You're probably hoping the hunters catch him.

TED: *Yes!* I don't know why. I have this weird life wish. It's our only hope unless you think he's gonna spit us out like Ol' Noah when he feels like it.

MAURA: Like who?

TED: Noah.

MAURA: Noah had the ark. Jonah was swallowed by the whale. Don't you know that?

TED: Sure, sure. Look, I made a mistake.

MAURA: It's a pretty big mistake. Jonah and Noah were pretty different people.

TED: Gabriel blew his horn and Daniel was in the lion's den. Satisfied?

MAURA: Who cut off Samson's hair?

TED: Leave the Bible quiz for somebody else, okay?

MAURA: You know, this is rather Biblical.

(Pause.)

TED: Yeah, hell gets mentioned quite a bit in the Bible.

MAURA: *(Pause.)* Do you think we might be dead?

TED: Oh, that makes me feel real good.

MAURA: This sure is impossible. And quite fantastic. Maybe we're in some celestial waiting station. Maybe we are dead.

TED: Not if I'm still hungry.

(She hands him some cookies still in their wrapper.)

MAURA: Here.

TED: You wouldn't have a walkie-talkie in there would you?

MAURA: Sorry. *(She takes articles out of her pants.)* Compass. Pen-knife—Swiss Army.

TED: Of course.

MAURA: With can opener attachment. Beans. My Jacques Cousteau book. Needle and thread.

TED: How come you're so well prepared? You a Girl Guide?

(He laughs.)

MAURA: A Brown Owl.

TED: Brown Owl?

MAURA: I'm the leader of Troop 144. Every Tuesday night at six-thirty. They're the nicest little girls. What a great, open age. They recycled newspapers so they could adopt a whale.

TED: Why are you a Brown Owl?

MAURA: It's something to do. Something I enjoy.

TED: Any of the Brownies yours?

MAURA: No.

TED: I've got two girls. They might be Brownies.

MAURA: You don't know?

TED: They live with their mother. You're sure a surprise. I didn't think your kind did things for people.

MAURA: What's that supposed to mean?

TED: You're so busy crying out for animals you forget about people.

MAURA: Is that true?

TED: The Brownies are probably a cover. I'll bet you have lots of stuffed animals and calendars with cats on them.

MAURA: No. Whales.

TED: Of course. And you probably work in a pet store.

MAURA: A hospital.

TED: Aha. An animal hospital.

MAURA: A people hospital. I'm a nurse.

TED: Oh, okay so I'm wrong, you do care about people.

MAURA: Do you?

TED: I guess so. When I have to.

(The flashlight goes out.)

MAURA: Oh no.

TED: You said it was good for hours and hours.

MAURA: Yes. They're the batteries in the toy that out-drums all the other toys.

TED: How long have they been in there?

MAURA: Three ... or four years.

TED: You're supposed to take batteries out when you're not using them.

MAURA: Ohhhhh. I hate this.

TED: *(He uses his lighter for some light.)* Lucky for you I have filthy habits.

MAURA: Oh thank goodness. I hate total darkness. I was in a cave tour once and when the guide had us at the very end of it he said, "We are now two kilometres from the mouth of the cave. Above us rises two and a half kilometres of mountain and rock." And then he turned off the lights and said, "This is total darkness. Your eyes will never adjust, it will always be this pitch black. Imagine if I left you here." And then he didn't talk anymore. Finally somebody said, *"Please the lights, the lights!"*

TED: Was that somebody you?

MAURA: I don't remember.

TED: Scared of the dark, eh?

MAURA: *Yes!*

TED: It doesn't bother me that much.

MAURA: That's why you flicked your Bic so quick.

TED: Okay, okay, so I don't like the dark either. It doesn't cast much light, does it?

MAURA: It casts something. *(Sings.)* "This little Brownie light of mine, I'm gonna let it shine."

TED: *Please.*

MAURA: It makes me feel better.

TED: It doesn't help me. I don't know it. I can't sing along.

MAURA: I'll teach it to you.

TED: No. It's too little girlie for me.

MAURA: How about this one? It's a spiritual. Now you sing: *Who did it? Who did?* Everytime I sing: *Who did swallow Jonah?* Ready, everybody. Here we go. *Who did swallow Jonah, Jonah, who did swallow Jonah, Jonah.* You're not singing.

TED: I know.

MAURA: *(Sings.)* Swallow Jonah, Jonah, who did swallow Jonah *uuuuuuppppppp!*

TED: Did you have to pick that song?

MAURA: It's simple to learn.

TED: Little too close to home, don't you think?

MAURA: It came to mind that's all.

TED: It must be one of your Greenpeace ditties.

MAURA: Yes. We sing it on bus trips. It's kind of our ninety-nine-bottles-of-beer-on-the-wall song. We keep changing the species of whale for the second verse. We'll go, "Whale did, whale did" then, "beluga did, beluga did" and, "humpback did, humpback did" and—

TED: I get the picture. It makes it an even stupider song. And I won't sing it.

(His Bic goes out.)   {unplug}

MAURA: Oh no oh no.

TED: You got any matches in those Israeli army pants?

MAURA: Yes. But they got wet.

TED: This is it then?

MAURA: Yesss.

TED: It's so dark.

MAURA: So dark.

(Pause. Then TED sings)

TED: *Who did? Who did? Who did swallow Noah, Noah.*

MAURA: *Jonah, Jonah.*

TED: *(Still singing.) Whoever you say, just keep singing. Who did? Who did?*

MAURA: *Who did swallow Jonah, Jonah?*

TED: *Who did, who did …*

MAURA: *Who did swallow Jonah, Jonah?*

TED: *Who did, who did …*

(As they sing on in the darkness the whale joins in their song. The end.)

Freedom Fighters

by Guillermo Verdecchia

Characters

BEN, the SENATOR, MARSHALL and a dancer.

Setting

The Alamo Corral and Tavern.

(Loud music and flashing lights. The SENATOR and BEN are sitting at a table.)

BEN: So this is The Conference Room.

SENATOR: This is it. The Inner Sanctum.

BEN: I always thought it would be a lot quieter. You know, one of those big long tables, overhead lighting, big ashtrays …

SENATOR: If you want something to stay a secret, yell it in the middle of a crowd.

BEN: Why would you do that, sir?

SENATOR: It's a saying, Ben. Look at us here—no one knows who we are—we're two regular guys having a drink and enjoying the scenery.

BEN: Scenery, sir?

SENATOR: The girls, Ben.

BEN: Of course. The scenery.

SENATOR: Nice kaboongas on that one, don't you think?

BEN: Which one, sir?

SENATOR: You do like girls, don't you, Ben?

BEN: Yes, sir.

SENATOR: Good. Nothing wrong with that. That's what made this country what it is today: Men with big hard dicks who like girls. Is your dick big, Ben?

BEN: Yes, sir.

SENATOR: Good. Always be prepared.

BEN: What's that sir?

SENATOR: Boy Scout motto.

BEN: Shouldn't we be getting down to work, sir?

SENATOR: Easy, son. Rome wasn't built in a day.

BEN: Yes, sir.

SENATOR: Now then. Hondorica.

BEN: Yes, sir. As I see it there are several options in terms of dealing with Pobray.

SENATOR: The bastard.

BEN: Yes, sir.

SENATOR: The slimy red pig dog. "Land reform." Damn commie pig dogs got tricky phrases for everything. Thief! Low down stinky stinky stinky toe licking, turkey-necked worm-faced, yellow-livered, buzzard sucking thief.

BEN: Who's that, sir?

SENATOR: That shit chewing, rabbit loving Pobray.

BEN: Yes, sir.

SENATOR: Now then, there's only one course of action. Somebody steals something from you, what do you do?

BEN: He didn't exactly steal the land from—

SENATOR: What are you talking about?

BEN: He did pay—

SENATOR: Pay? He paid what's on the books. Unified Banana is worth fifty times what it says its worth on paper. We have to protect Unified Banana because what's good for Unified Banana is good for America and the other way around as well. Now, you'll take your orders directly from me.

BEN: Yes, sir.

SENATOR: The following people are also involved in the operation. Johnny Dull.

BEN: Secretary of State.

SENATOR: And legal counsel for UniBan.

BEN: Uniban, sir?

SENATOR: Code for Unified Banana.

BEN: Yes, sir.

SENATOR: Also involved are: Johnny's brother, Al.

BEN: Director of CIA.

SENATOR: And legal counsel for Uniban. Also Annie Whiteman.

BEN: The President's secretary?

SENATOR: Her husband is director of public relations for Uniban. Then there's John the Butcher.

BEN: The Butcher?

SENATOR: Nickname. He's ambassador to Hondorica.

BEN: I didn't know we had one. He could be very useful. Does he speak Spanish?

SENATOR: No. He's American.

BEN: I see.

SENATOR: Don't worry. We've got somebody lined up to do all the Spanish speaking we need.

BEN: Who's that, sir?

SENATOR: The next President of Hondorica: Lieutenant Colonel General Pianissimo Marshall Raoul. He should be here now actually. Crazy spics, never on time.

BEN: What about the President, sir?

SENATOR: Our President?

BEN: Yes, sir.

SENATOR: He doesn't speak Spanish either.

BEN: That's not what I meant, sir.

SENATOR: What did you mean?

BEN: Does he know?

SENATOR: Know what?

BEN: About Operation Liberty Freedom Save the Bananas.

SENATOR: Of course he does. The President knows everything. He's impotent.

BEN: He's what, sir?

SENATOR: Impotent, son. The President of the United States is impotent.

BEN: He is?

SENATOR: He certainly is. Just like the Pope.

BEN: The Pope?

SENATOR: Sure. Whada they call it? He can't make a mistake. Papal impotency. He knows everything. Just like the President.

BEN: Omnipotent? Omniscient?

SENATOR: What are saying?

BEN: Infallible.

SENATOR: You watch your mouth there, boy. That's the President you're talking about. Hey, there's Marshall. Marshall, over here, hombre! You're late, amigo!

MARSHALL: Uncle Joe. *(They hug.)*

SENATOR: Marshall, it's good to see your ugly mug. Let me introduce you to my right hand, Ben Birch.

MARSHALL: It's a pleasure to meet you.

SENATOR: We were just discussing your coming home party.

MARSHALL: Ah, you Americanos. Always business. You never relax.

SENATOR: Can't relax, Marshall. Too busy saving the world from itself.

BEN: The Senator has told me a lot about you.

MARSHALL: Has he? Did he tell you how we would argue in his class? Uncle Joe was the best teacher I ever had in the School of the Americas.

BEN: I didn't know you taught there.

SENATOR: Sure did. Marshall was my worst student. He'll be handling the actual transfer of power in Hondorica for us.

BEN: That's swell of you, Marsh. You're averting a Soviet beach-head in our backyard.

MARSHALL: The tentacles of the Kremlin are plain to see, aren't they? They must be cut, severed, hacked off, bludgeoned, pulverized, mutilated, amputated, demolished, ripped out by their roots, and incinerated. Hondorica must be free.

SENATOR: You Latinos—so melodramatic.

MARSHALL: To you it is a melodrama. To me it is real. Hondorica is infected and there must be a cleansing of the blood. The tears of mothers will redeem the country.

BEN: Maybe we could discuss some operational details?

MARSHALL: Everything will go wonderfully. The Archbishop is praying for us.

SENATOR: Never hurts.

BEN: I have a couple of tactical questions—

MARSHALL: Everything will work out. Hondorica has no planes or anti-aircraft machinery. Your planes will encounter no resistance when they drop their bombs.

SENATOR: Marshall, you've thought it all through. You make me proud.

MARSHALL: Gentlemen, let us turn our thoughts to gentler things. Myself, I wish to enjoy your good American air. It smells of freedom.

ALL: To freedom.

(They drink.)

MARSHALL: To the flag.

ALL: To the flag.

(They drink.)

SENATOR: To democracy.

ALL: Democracy.

(They drink.)

BEN: From the Greek: *demos*, "to the people" and *kratis* "to rule." I think.

MARSHALL: Rule by the people as in the Athenian model. Greek society was a noble one but it retained some oligarchic elements. In the American model, the Greatest Good extends to the entire populace. I will give you a concrete example.

(He exits.)

SENATOR: I taught him everything he knows.

BEN: He's a swell guy.

(MARSHALL returns with a dancer who begins a table dance.)

MARSHALL: In Greece, there were many privileges reserved for the rich. In America, those privileges are available to all. Democracy, gentlemen, is a two dollar table dance.

(Blackout. The end.)

"It's all make believe, isn't it?"
—Marilyn Monroe

by Sharon Pollock

Characters

SHE and PAT.

Setting

A kitchen.

(SHE sits at the kitchen table wearing a white terry-cloth robe tightly belted; its length is mid-calf. SHE has nothing on under the robe. Her feet are bare. A large thesaurus is on the table. SHE's reading from it, her index finger following the print. PAT, a young athletic woman of about thirty, leans against the kitchen counter, smoking a cigarette, and watching her.)

SHE: Meat … meat flesh game food fare.

PAT: You should have some.

SHE: Some what?

PAT: Some food, you should have some food.

SHE: Shut-up. Meat—food fare eats chow grub kernel pith nub heart …

(Pause.) Heart! *(She laughs and shakes her head back and forth as She repeats.)* Heart, heart ... Hard! Marrow! Stuff! Sum! Substance! Stim-u-lating! Stimulating suggestive profound pointed pregnant ... *(Whispers.)* Pregnant. *(Pause.)* Where's my book? ... Where's my book!

PAT: In the bedroom?

SHE: Don't ask me. I don't know! Get my book! ... Get my book get my book get my fucking book! Nooow! *(SHE watches PAT leave the room, then returns to the thesaurus.)* Meaningful ... Significant ... *(SHE looks up from the book, looks in the direction of PAT's exit and yells after her.)* Immoral! Vicious! Fallen! Untrustworthy, corrupt, and you will find all that under the antonym for naive trusting unaffected candid wholesome natural naked nude stripped exposed defenseless!

(SHE snatches a small red diary from PAT who has returned.)

PAT: I don't think so.

SHE: *(As she writes in the diary.)* No, you never think, do you. Vulnerable powerless, how do you spell that?

PAT: Spell what?

SHE: W-h-a-t. Gotcha. *(She laughs.)* What don't you think, come on tell me I wanna know, what doncha think?

PAT: I'd find them under antonyms for "naive."

SHE: Well what the fuck would you know, you don't know anything. If you knew anything you wouldn't have this crummy job, would you? Or is this a good job? It's a good job. A Good Job! We all want a Good Job, we all wanna good hand job, that's what we want. And you do a Good Job, doncha? I do a hand job and you do a good job handlin' the blonde bitch baby cunning sly helpless pamper pet Cosset!

PAT: Do you want something to eat?

SHE: No, I don't want anything to eat, coruscate, comes after corrupt, it's a verb, sparkle glitter gleam glare glow flicker ... flicker ... flicker is different, isn't it, flicker is on ... and off ... and on ... and off. And on and off *andonandoffandonandoff* ... Where is he?

PAT: I don't know.

SHE: You lie, everyone lies ... You know, I was thinking the other day, I was thinking—you wanna know what I was thinking?

PAT: You want a sandwich?

SHE: No, I don't wanna sandwich.

PAT: A hamburger?

SHE: No, I don't wanna hamburger.

PAT: How about an omelet?

SHE: I don't wanna an omelet.

PAT: A herb omelet.

SHE: I don't want anything to eat! Watch the lips, no nothing none nahnah nahnah nahnah! … Christ. *(SHE watches PAT open the fridge and stand looking in it.)* Are you gonna eat?

PAT: I might.

SHE: I don't wanna eat, don't want anything to eat … You wanna know what I was thinking? The other day? When I was thinking?

PAT: *(Closes the fridge door.)* So what were you thinking?

SHE: I dunno. I was thinkin' something. I was thinkin' … a woman must have to love a man with all her heart … to have his child … especially when she's not married to him and … when a man leaves a woman … when she tells him she's gonna have his baby … when he doesn't marry her … that must hurt a woman, very much, deep, down inside … and I was thinkin' I think this whole fuckin' house is bugged and the telephone, too. What do you think?

PAT: What makes you think that?

SHE: Where is he?

PAT: I don't know.

SHE: He said he'd come, he's a liar too … and you wanna know what else I was thinkin'? Do you?

PAT: What?

SHE: I was thinkin' I don't even know who I am, it's all make believe, isn't it, and I don't know who you are and I don't even know who Eunice is.

PAT: She's the housekeeper.

SHE: I know that! You think I'm stupid? Is that what you think? I'm not stupid, I'll tell you what's stupid, stupid is thinkin' you can pass people round like a piece a meat and throw 'em away like a piece a garbage, that's what stupid is and I am not stupid!

PAT: Do you want your pills?

SHE: *(A nasal imitation.)* No, I don't want my pills.

PAT: Do you want to lie down?

SHE: No, I don't wanna lie down, I don't wanna do anything. I wanna read my book, make notes, refresh my memory, improve my mind, you think my mind needs improving, don't you? ... Don't you? *(Pause.)* Where's Eunice?

PAT: She's out.

SHE: She's out. Eunice is out. Where's Eunice, Eunice is out, now I know, thank you so much Miss Newcombe, you are a fount of information. Why's she out, where is she? Eunice doesn't *gooo out!* Why is Eunice out? ... Eunice is out, Eunice is out to lunch! ... Although it is not lunch, what time is it? I tried to call Joey but I couldn't get a holda Joey so ... I'll talk to Joey later, and I tried to call Jack but the fuckin' switchboard won't put the call through and the number he gave me's gone disconnected no good any more'nd ... and ... I called San Francisco, called the hotel but he's not there, he's in L.A., isn't he? He's here, isn't he? You can tell me, tell me.

PAT: What makes you think the telephone's bugged?

SHE: Please.

PAT: What makes you think—

SHE: I'd bug it wouldn't you? Question is who, who'd bug it. Tap it, house is bugged, telephone's tapped. I'm fffrightened. I know too much. Like in the movies, it's all make believe, isn't it? I write everythin' down. Believed him. I believed him. Trusted. I dunno why. Like in the movies I should know better. Forget the name of the movie, lotsa movies 'bout that. Everyone thinks I'm crazy. Make believe. Tol' everybody. At the Lodge. Every fuckin' body. I told them Ole Frank and Johnny Roselli and Sam Giancana I said I ... know. He talks. In bed. I listen. Me. Listen. And guess what I hear? Guess!

PAT: Who'd want to bug the house?

SHE: Hoffa! The CIA! The FBI! The boss of bosses Sam Giancana! How about Hoover he hates Bobby's guts! Christ you live in Hollywood use your imagination I thought you worked for a fuckin' press agent who do you work for anyway?!

PAT: I work for you.

SHE: You work for him don't you ... Where's Eunice?

PAT: She's out.

SHE: Is he coming?

PAT: Who?

SHE: I love him! You can tell me, please I had his baby, here, inside, they scooped it out and threw it away in the garbage, he said he'd marry me, and now, now "no phone calls pul-ease!" and it's over and 'cept that 'n unstable 'n disintegrating and I'll tell you what's unstable and disintegrating is that whole fucking clan, him and his brother and the horse they rode in on! 'Cause you know what I'll tell you what their "intimate relationship" is gonna be on the front page of every fuckin' paper in the world and it's not only gonna be my name up there it's gonna be Bobby and Jack married to the mob so how do you like that so you can tell him that 'cause it's all in here! I wrote it down! Connections! P'lit'cal! ... Tell him I love him.

PAT: Do you want your pills?

SHE: Don' want any, make him come. *(PAT looks at her watch.)* Is he coming?

PAT: You should eat something.

SHE: Didcha ... set up ... t' press conference? Didcha? You didn't, didcha. Who do you work for, don' work for me, don' work for agen', you said you set up t' press conference! I tol' you to! I want it! Blow the lid offa—all the lies lies lies! Where's Eunice, Eunice isn't here, I'm scared, I'm frightened inside. *(PAT glances out the kitchen window.)* What is it? ... Who's there? Is ... is someone in the driveway, who is it? *(She joins PAT at the window.)* It's him. I knew he'd come, I knew it. Oh Pat, Pat keep him here, I gotta, my hair, oh God I love him, I knew he'd come, he wouldn't leave me like that!

(SHE starts to run into the bedroom.)

PAT: He's brought someone with him.

SHE: Who? *(Pause.)* Who'd he bring with him? Who?

PAT: Someone.

SHE: *(Whispers.)* Where's Eunice?

(The kitchen door opens.)

(Whispers.) Bobby? Please don't.

(Blackout. The end.)

Playing With Angels

by Donn Short

Characters

JESS: A woman in her thirties, married to Cal.
CAL: A man in his thirties, married to Jess.

Setting

Peterborough, Ontario. Jess and Cal's bedroom;
the present, night time.

(JESS is sitting alone in the room. CAL enters. He watches her for a moment. She does not notice him. At length, he walks over to the window.)

JESS: No, don't open it. Don't open the window, please. Don't let it out.

CAL: Let what out?

JESS: This moment. Just this very moment.

CAL: Jess, you're talking foolishness.

(JESS holds up a finger to bring silence to the room and keeps it raised for just a moment.)

JESS: Did you ever feel that you were just a finger and a thumb away from totally changing your life, just … one decision or a single act away from *(Clenches her fist.) choking* the breath out of what you call your life?

CAL: You need air.

JESS: *Don't* open that window … I remember once at Western, second year I think, sitting in Professor Sacker's office not listening to a word he said. The entire time, I was thinking about what he'd do if I reached over and kissed him. And you know, just sitting there, thinking that, while he talked … I blushed. That's how real it was to me, just thinking about it. Just this far away from kissing him.

CAL: *(Doesn't really want to ask.)* What made you think of doing that … kissing him?

JESS: Just to see. Just to see what happens after you do something. *(Sighs.)* I've already done that though, seen what happens … after. I don't mean with Professor Sacker.

CAL: I'm not going to ask you what you're talking about.

JESS: Something … and what happens after you do something. You already know what I'm talking about.

CAL: It's hot. If you don't want the window open then I'm going for a walk.

JESS: Stay.

CAL: Jess, I can't breathe in here.

JESS: You're here now, I don't want you to disturb this room by leaving.

> *(CAL begins to pace. He continues to pace throughout the remainder of the play as though trapped.)*

CAL: I repeat, you make no sense. I don't know what—

JESS: We both know. Neither one of us is saying it.

CAL: All right, all right! Barbara's back. Barbara Fontaine is back. Is that it? Barbara's back! So what? What's that got to do with us?

> *(JESS gives him a long look. It fairly makes him wither away.)*

What the hell is she doing here anyway? Jesus Christ there's nothing for her here in Peterborough!

JESS: How quaint you are Cal. Do you really ask that? Why is Barbara here? This is *life!* … She doesn't need a reason to be here. She's *here!* The question now is what are we going to—don't … open … that … window.

CAL: It's your question, you answer it. I'm looking away from it.

JESS: No, no. I looked away before. The neighbours, though, they n-e-e-ver stopped looking right at it ... talking over and under it. After the fire, after the house burned down, the city put boards up so you couldn't see any more where the house used to be. Except for one little hole you could look through.

(She curves her fingers over her thumb, forming a "hole in the fence." She looks through it for a long moment.)

Everybody said what a tragedy it was that an entire family was taken in one night, and of course it was. But nobody talked about the parents, as if they were somehow incidental. They were just thinking of the kids. I liked Mr. Fontaine most of all. He gave me some tadpoles once ... put 'em in an empty tin can full of water and tore the label off, but I remember it was Del Monte Green Beans. They didn't build another house on the lot. I guess nobody would live in such a house. They put up a parking garage though—okay to park your car there.

CAL: There are mine fields in this room. I'm asking you nothing.

JESS: Barbara went to live with her grandmother after. I visited once, only once 'cause that's all that ... what's proper asks for. That old lady kept pictures of the kids, I mean pictures of them in their coffins, on the living room wall and made Barbara look at 'em every night before she went to bed. "Still family," she'd say. "Still your brothers and sisters." Crazy. Everybody talked about the loss but what they meant was the two kids ... I don't ever remember anybody mentioning Mister or Mrs. Fontaine ... I liked Mr. Fontaine.

(CAL moves to the window, looks out.)

I think that's when I realized I had no idea how old Barbara was. She always seemed to be ... no age.

(CAL looks at her. If she goes on, he'll listen. That's as far as he'll go.)

I asked her once. "How old are you?" "I don't know." That was her answer—"I don't know." I can't say it the same way she did. "I don't know." How old are you? "I don't know." No matter what tone I use, it sounds fake or pretentious and nothing about her was either. How old are you? "I don't know. I don't know." I still can't say it the way she did. But I can hear it, I can hear it.

(JESS moves to the coat rack, but CAL blocks her way.)

CAL: Do you know what would happen if you went to her ... and spoke?

Your face is not a place to hide secrets, Jess. I can see what you want to do, what you want to tell her.

(JESS turns completely away.)

Turn away and I see it written in your shoulders. Do you really think you can recast yourself into the image of you that dances in your head? By speaking? You'd never find the words—you're a creature of inner thoughts, Jess. You sit alone in rooms and think. You exist inside yourself, nobody knows who you are but you. I don't care what's in there. I never did. I want what I recognize, not what you think you are. Go ahead, walk into the fantasy version of yourself that only you can see anyway. Be something else. Would anybody even notice?

(JESS moves further down stage.)

But if you change, Jess, then we change. I can't promise you I'll want you different ... probably I won't. Are we happy? I don't know. I've never asked the question and I'm not asking it now. Do you have the courage to face what we'll become, Jess, if you tell her? Will the new you be that fearless? You did nothing, do nothing now. Trust the instinct not to act, Jess.

JESS: *(After a pause.)* My father grew apart from his children by doing nothing.

CAL: You did nothing.

JESS: *(Putting on a scarf.)* I lied to her until I lied to myself.

CAL: *(Nothing else is working.)* I love you, Jess.

JESS: Lie to me, Cal.

CAL: I love you.

JESS: Lie to me again.

CAL: I love you.

JESS: Lie to me.

CAL: I love you Jess.

JESS: *(Tired, resigned.)* Lie to me more. Tell me it wasn't me who put the penny in the fuse box. Tell me it wasn't me who did that. Tell me Barbara hasn't lived her whole life blaming the memory of her father for something I did. Tell me.

CAL: I remember nothing.

JESS: Funny. I remember a party I can't let go of. In that wonderful old house Mr. Fontaine was so proud of. An engagement party, for us. So much happy noise that night—music and laughter upstairs and downstairs, every radio in the house on. And two record players. Imagine a house with two record players. And then the lights went out. The power … just went out. I was almost proud—our party had blown a fuse. And then. I remember seeing you and Barbara standing in the darkness … at *our* engagement party … and your asking me to go to the store to buy a new fuse. What was it about the way you asked me to do that? No. I wasn't going to leave the two of you alone for need of a forty-cent fuse. So I struck a bargain with the devil that night and saved myself thirty-nine cents. Just one penny in the fuse box and magic!—Black magic … lights again, music again, and you and Barbara no longer alone in the darkness. But you remember nothing. Tell me one more lie, Cal. Tell me two days later Barbara's house didn't burn down. They blamed Mr. Fontaine for putting that penny in the fuse box. I liked Mr. Fontaine … You and I never spoke up, never told anybody … that it was really me. And we got each other. Tell me, Cal. Tell me about the good time, the life-long happiness we bought for a penny.

CAL: *(After a pause.)* I love what we have and I don't want us changed. That's enough, that's enough for me. I'd be grateful for that. Wake up to it, Jess, it's the struggle of any two people trying to last and it has nothing to do with being happy, don't be so arrogant.

JESS: Barbara's parents … Mr. Fontaine …

CAL: … are dead.

JESS: Her little brother and sister …

CAL: *(Shakes his head slowly.)* They're playing with angels.

JESS: Barbara …

CAL: … will never heal by anything you can tell her.

    (JESS shudders.)

What else is there?

    (JESS puts her hand to her face, looks again through the "hole in the fence.")

JESS: Absolution.

CAL: *(Pulling her hand away.)* Fight to stay the same, Jess.

    (JESS moves away from him.)

Isn't that enough? Let me open the window, Jess. Jess? … Jess?

    (JESS doesn't answer, she doesn't move. The end.)

Landscape With Pigeons

Dedicated to the memory of Jay Dorff.

by Mark Owen

Characters

MARGUERITE: Marguerite Decrett is in her seventies but looks fifty and is every inch a society lady. Her big claim to fame is that she was once married to a Canadian diplomat and minor politician. She is divorced, lives in Ottawa and speaks with a slight, French accent. She has money.

LILY: Lily Mosby is a middle-class mother from Hamilton. She's slightly overweight, in her early sixties but looks older. She's tired, poor, bitter and very straight forward. She has a tendency to only hear what she wants to.

Setting

A bench in Stuyvesant Park in front of Beth Israel
Hospital, New York. It is late winter, 1992.

(LILY is sitting on a bench, feeding pigeons popcorn, the micro-wave-able kind that come in vending machines. She's exhausted, and looks blank. After a moment MARGUERITE enters, she's

wearing a fur coat. She walks directly in front of LILY disturbing all the pigeons, who fly away. MARGUERITE sits, she's smoking. LILY empties her entire bag of popcorn onto the ground and throws the bag away. Pause.)

MARGUERITE: I'm sorry about Paul.

LILY: Paul? Paul Mosby Jr.? The one named after his father? Is that who you're referring to?

MARGUERITE: It's nice to finally meet, Lily. I'm Marguerite.

LILY: How do you know who I am?

MARGUERITE: I'm Alain's mother. Paul spoke of you often. I'm very glad you were able to make it down. I saw you in the hospital and followed you out.

LILY: Too late the hero, eh? So you finally get to meet the shrew. Are you satisfied?

MARGUERITE: No. I don't think you're a shrew.

LILY: Lucky me.

(Pause.)

MARGUERITE: Have you been to New York before?

LILY: Came here once in 1973 on a bus trip as a chaperon with the school band. My boy used to play saxophone in the band. Must have spent a fortune on getting him all those private lessons. But I always wanted for him what his father and I didn't have. He never did appreciate that. No, I must say I never have liked big cities; Hamilton always suited me fine. Could never understand why my son would want to live here.

MARGUERITE: I've always loved New York. I used to come quite frequently until Alain met Paul. When they moved in together, Alain changed—in his attitude—towards me. I remember once, after they'd moved in, I had booked a suite at the Sherry Netherland and had expected Alain to come and stay with me as he always had—when he refused I was distraught for days.

LILY: Never did listen to me. Thought I was just some old broad bossing him around. Never could understand for all his fancy education and friends that I knew him better than he ever gave me credit for.

MARGUERITE: I wish it hadn't taken me so long to accept who Alain had chosen to love.

LILY: *(Deliberately changing the subject.)* What's your son do?

MARGUERITE: *(Slightly startled by the abrupt change in subject.)* Architect. His father wanted him to be a lawyer. But he's done very well. I'm hoping, now, that he may move back to Canada.

LILY: Once, a long time ago, I gave birth to a little boy. That was the happiest moment of my life. And for many years after that I brought him up, fed him and changed him, his father too, eh. We loved him, in the only way we knew how.

MARGUERITE: Children, it's so hard to know what the right thing to do is anymore.

LILY: After school he moved down here, to become a famous artist. What a joke, eh? We always thought it was a mistake. I mean you tell me, here's this guy, with no money, and we certainly didn't have any to give him, not like you. So here he is fresh out of Art School, being all rebellious and all and he wants to move to New York to be an artist. We—his father and I—we just couldn't support him in something we believed in our hearts was so wrong minded. Why couldn't he get a job, get married like everyone else—but no, oh no, he had to be different.

MARGUERITE: Our sons loved each other very much.

LILY: I shouldn't be rambling on to you like this. Nice lady like yourself doesn't want to be hearing my troubles.

MARGUERITE: No, it's good. Two Canadian women, meet in a park in front of a hospital in New York City. Our lives have been intertwined for years yet we have never met or spoken. It's like something out of a Margaret Atwood novel.

LILY: Lotta good talkings gonna do now. I hated my son, hated him for what he was, for what he wasn't. For what he's done to us. It's not easy you know.

MARGUERITE: I do.

LILY: My son died here early this morning. On the fourth floor of that Jewish hospital behind us. Of course I wanted to come right away but I couldn't afford the plane ticket, you know when you don't buy those goddamn things way in advance, they cost an arm and a leg, so I took the bus down Friday night, got in this morning and rushed over here. His father wasn't much inclined to let me come—but men, they don't understand what it's like to be a mother.

MARGUERITE: No, they don't.

LILY: Our son was very mean to us. He just stopped talking to us years ago, just because we didn't understand his "lifestyle." It's not so easy to change like people expect you to. I was born and bred in the east end of Hamilton, Ontario, hardly what you might call an enlightened place. In my day we would have thrown people like him in jail. Now, of course, they march down the street parading around like it's natural. Well, I'm sorry my boy is dead but I still believe that if he had only changed his ways none of this would have happened. I'm sorry if I seem mean spirited to you but my tears have all but dried up years ago. Besides I don't care what you think anyway.

MARGUERITE: That's good. Strength is a good thing. I just wanted you to know that I do care very deeply. I can't imagine what it must be like to lose a son. A child that you gave birth to, loved ... Listen, it's getting chilly out here, can I buy you lunch? There's a nice restaurant not far from here.

LILY: No, thanks. I think that I'd like to just sit here with the pigeons.

MARGUERITE: Well, I won't bother you any more. I just wanted to meet you. Also, there was one thing—I wanted to tell you how special a person your son was—to me and my son. I got to know him over the last little while and I regret that I had been so stubborn, so resistant for so long. He was a wonderful man. You should be proud.

LILY: *(Not really to anyone in particular.)* He was a good boy. I just don't know what happened.

MARGUERITE: Are you sure that I can't ...

LILY: I just want to be left alone.

> *(There is a very long pause. MARGUERITE does not move, but sits quietly by LILY's side.)*

Why don't you just get out of here? You don't know anything about me or my life. Go back to your hoity-toity world. I did what I had to do. You don't know what it's like. He was our only son. We wanted grandchildren, a family that lived close by, not some artsy-fartsy fairy living in New York City who was too good to even come home for Christmas. Why should we change? We're too old to change. Why did he have to talk about it all the time? Talk about his "lover"— especially in front of his father, who was sickened by the whole thing, but who never said anything about it because it was his son. If he'd just been quiet about it ... Life is suffering for some, Marguerite—but you wouldn't know about that, would you? You're son is still alive.

(Pause. MARGUERITE collects herself in silence and goes to leave but stops short and turns to look at LILY one more time.)

MARGUERITE: Your son wanted to be cremated. If you would like to see where he lived or meet his lover of eight years, my son, then you are more than welcome to. Here. *(She hands LILY a card.)* This has our address and phone number on it. Paul had requested that his ashes be spread into the ocean off the beach at Fire Island. Alain was thinking that he would like to do that this summer, when the weather is better. You see, Lily, Alain and Paul used to rent a house together and play and make love and have a life by the sea, each summer for eight years. They both want to be cremated and sprinkled into the sea, the place that gave them such joy when they were both well. I followed you here today to ask you to come and do this with us. At my expense, please. I suppose I was wrong but I—it's just that … I know in the not-too-distant future, I will be doing the same for Alain and I thought maybe you could get to know him like I have gotten to know your son and then we could go down to the ocean together. For our children.

(Pause. MARGUERITE walks off never once turning to look at LILY. LILY picks up the bag that contained the popcorn, places some of the popcorn back into the bag and resumes feeding the pigeons. The end.)

Fear

by Greg Nelson

Characters

SMITH and JONES are of either sex.

Setting

A public place.

(SMITH and JONES are alone. JONES is studying several sheets of paper.)

SMITH: Excuse me.

JONES: Yes?

SMITH: I'm frightened.

JONES: Sorry?

SMITH: I'm frightened.

(Slight pause.)

JONES: Uh …

SMITH: I'm supposed to tell someone. If I acknowledge it and name it and put it into words then I can begin to heal. My wounds of fear can begin to heal. Do you mind?

JONES: Of course not.

SMITH: Thank you. I don't want to impose.

JONES: Not at all.

SMITH: Thank you.

> *(Pause.)*

JONES: What are you frightened of?

SMITH: I'm not exactly sure.

JONES: Oh.

SMITH: Which is frightening, don't you think?

JONES: Yes.

SMITH: You do?

JONES: Yes, I do.

SMITH: I haven't been sleeping much either. Everytime I close my eyes the world starts spinning. Which is ironic I mean because that's what it's doing right? Spinning.

JONES: Yes.

SMITH: I mean it's actually spinning. The entire world is spinning all the time.

JONES: Right.

SMITH: That's what it's doing.

JONES: On it's axis.

SMITH: That's right, on it's axis, that's right. Spinning.

JONES: Yes.

> *(Longer pause. JONES goes back to reading.)*

SMITH: People don't think anymore.

JONES: Sorry?

SMITH: They don't. They just sit around and, and watch TV. Why don't people think?

JONES: Well—

SMITH: When was the last time you saw somebody really thinking about something, I mean *really* really thinking, I don't mean making a choice, like at the store, I mean actually using their *mind*, actually thinking about some kind of major philosophical or ethical *dilemma*.

JONES: I can't remember.

SMITH: You don't see that anymore. I mean people didn't used to go to movies. They used to go to, you know, four-hour-long political debates, you know, sitting there eating their popcorn. Hundred years ago, your average sentence was like a *paragraph* long, today what are they?

JONES: Well—

SMITH: Couple of words. Headlines. People don't read anymore.

JONES: That's true.

SMITH: They, they, they, they glance.

JONES: Yes.

SMITH: People, when they have voices in their heads, they're not *their* voices, they're like Bill Cosby, or, or Oprah, or that guy on the CBC. I mean when they think. Their thoughts. People aren't thinking their own thoughts, that's what I'm saying, they're letting Oprah do their thinking for them, and not just Oprah, Oprah's voice, they're thinking with Oprah's voice, which isn't even thinking, I mean those aren't thoughts, they're just voices they're like, like, meaningless voices, I mean that's not thinking. Why isn't anyone thinking?

JONES: I don't know.

SMITH: I personally only watch the news channel. And only then when I can't sleep. Once I get started watching it usually I can't stop, because I get sort of hypnotized by all the pretty colours. And then suddenly it's morning and I still haven't slept and the world's still spinning.

JONES: Look—

SMITH: I've been doing some research and frankly I don't give this world ten years. I give it five. Five years. Because we're locked inside this self-destructing system and its going to eat us all alive. Because we can't stop it, we've thrown away the key, we have to wait for it to run it's course, until it drags us down, our entire civilization, until it destroys us, consumes us, sucks us into the black hole of profit and Greed-with-a-capital-"G" until some day soon somebody's going to light a match and the whole thing goes up. The whole thing. All of it. It goes up.

(JONES gives a nervous laugh.)

It's not funny.

JONES: No, I—

SMITH: Nobody laughs when they're dead.

(Pause.)

JONES: Do you work for the government?

SMITH: What?

JONES: You look familiar.

SMITH: What?

JONES: I work for the government. I thought perhaps I might have seen you somewhere. In the corridors.

(Pause. SMITH looks at JONES.)

SMITH: You work for the government?

JONES: That's right. I type things into computers.

SMITH: Oh.

JONES: Secret things.

SMITH: Oh.

JONES: There are specific rules. I must not read what I type. I must not understand what I type. I must not remember what I type. After I am finished I must shred what I type.

SMITH: Shred …

JONES: Yes, in the shredder. But I don't. For several years now I have in fact refrained from shredding. I have kept these secret documents. I have taken them home and I have read them.

SMITH: Oh.

JONES: And I have developed a theory.

(JONES looks around, cautiously, then speaks confidentially to SMITH.)

I believe these documents are issued at the very top. I believe these papers are the s*ource*.

SMITH: The source?

JONES: The *source*.

SMITH: Oh what?

JONES: Of *everything*.

SMITH: I see.

JONES: And this is the result. *(Gestures around.)* All of this. This world. Trees, cars, buildings, people, thoughts, *deeds*, all have their source in these papers. Nothing happens by chance. Everything has been antici-pated, indeed, *directed* by these papers.

SMITH: Everything?

JONES: *Everything.* I believe these papers are the *key.* I believe that if you could read these papers, you could understand for example your *fears*, and, having understood them, you could calm them.

SMITH: If I could ...

JONES: These papers, yes.

(They look at the papers.)

Would you like to have a glance? Would you like to read them?

SMITH: Yes.

(JONES gives SMITH the papers. SMITH tries to read them, fails. Tries again, fails again.)

JONES: Well?

SMITH: I can't read them.

JONES: What?

SMITH: They don't make any sense.

JONES: You can't read them?

SMITH: No.

JONES: Not at all?

SMITH: *(Frightened.)* They don't make any sense.

(JONES takes the papers back.)

What do they say?

(No answer.)

Can you understand them?

(No answer.)

Oh my God. You can't understand them either?

(JONES shakes head.)

Oh my God. That's frightening. I mean I find that really terrifying. Really. Isn't that terrifying?

JONES: Yes. Yes it is.

(Long pause.)

SMITH: Sometimes I get the feeling that everything I say has been said before. By someone else. Do you ever get that feeling?

JONES: Yes.

(The end.)

Fade to Black

by David Gillies

Characters

BOB and a STAGE MANAGER, female.

Setting

A bare stage.

(The lights go out. In the darkness the sound of a horrendous car accident is heard. The lights come up to reveal BOB illuminated softly in a special light. He is sitting bolt upright in a puritanical straight backed chair. He stares straight ahead with an expression of uncomprehending horror on his face. He maintains this expression and posture for a fairly long time and then we hear the earthy female voice of the STAGE MANAGER. Her only presence in the play is as a voice-over.)

STAGE MANAGER: Bob? *(Pause.)* Bob? *(Pause.)* Bob!

BOB: *(As if coming out of a trance.)* Yes?

STAGE MANAGER: Ah, good, now you can hear me.

BOB: Yes.

STAGE MANAGER: How are you feeling?

BOB: Feeling? I don't know. Strangely ambivalent.

STAGE MANAGER: That's good.

BOB: It is?

STAGE MANAGER: Yes. It means you don't remember anything.

BOB: Remember what? Where am I? Who are you?

STAGE MANAGER: A few moments ago you were in a serious car accident.

BOB: Get out.

STAGE MANAGER: It's true, Bob.

BOB: What the hell is going on?

STAGE MANAGER: Don't fight it.

BOB: I ... I remember ... I was just in my car ... I was on my way to the office ...

STAGE MANAGER: You were on the freeway. You were talking on the cellular phone ...

BOB: Yes! I was calling the office ... and then ... and then ...

STAGE MANAGER: You tried to light a cigarette.

BOB: That's right!

STAGE MANAGER: Bad move, Bob.

BOB: What do you mean, "bad move"? Jesus Christ! What's that semi doing there?

STAGE MANAGER: You wandered over the center line ...

BOB: The truck went right over me.

STAGE MANAGER: Doesn't it blow your mind what a semi-trailer can do to a small car.

BOB: And then ... I don't remember anything after that.

STAGE MANAGER: I guess not.

BOB: But, hey, I'm okay, right. Not a scratch ... *(Checking himself.)* Everybody says I was born with a horseshoe up my ass. Hell, I can always buy another car. *(Laughs crazily, looks at his watch.)* Holy crow! I gotta go. *(He scrambles about looking for the door.)* Is there a phone somewhere? Where's the door? How the hell do you get out of here? Dammit! I need a goddamn phone! Hey! You! The voice! I'm already having a very bad day. Why are you trying to make it worse? Maybe you don't understand. I'm a very busy man. I have an important meeting I should have been at five minutes ago. Am I being charged with a traffic offense here? If that's what this is all about, could we please get on with it. Come on! There's a million-dollar deal riding on this. *(Pause.)* Oh, what the hell.

(BOB slumps in the chair.)

STAGE MANAGER: Bob? You there?

BOB: Finally. I have to get out of here.

STAGE MANAGER: Bob, we have to talk. I'm afraid I have some bad news.

BOB: This entire day is bad news.

STAGE MANAGER: I'm afraid you're not doing very well.

BOB: I know! I can't even find a phone!

STAGE MANAGER: It doesn't matter, Bob. You did terrible damage to your material body when you drove under the truck. I'm afraid, your body's dead.

BOB: Are you nuts?

STAGE MANAGER: Accept it.

BOB: I'm right here. What's this dead crap?

STAGE MANAGER: Use your common sense, Bob. You don't really think you survived that crash without a scratch?

BOB: But I did! Didn't I! Sure, it happens. Hell, people fall out of airplanes and survive. Sure, I remember hitting the steering column … and the roof collapsing … Oh, god … what happened to me? I remember a hot white flash … and then nothing. Oh, boy … I got crunched, didn't I?

STAGE MANAGER: Try not to dwell on it. It's over. It's finished. You're history, Bob. Look on the bright side. You worked steadily for thirty-six years. Not many actors can say that.

BOB: That's it? So sudden? One second I'm driving an $80,000 sports car, the next second I'm here.

STAGE MANAGER: That's the way it works.

BOB: It's not fair!

STAGE MANAGER: Talk to your agent.

BOB: How long do I have to stay here?

STAGE MANAGER: That depends. You may be assigned another role.

BOB: Wait a minute … actor? *(Laughs crazily.)* Agent? What are you talking about?

STAGE MANAGER: You're going to have to make a major adjustment in your … expectations.

BOB: *(Pacing the room.)* What is this? The afterlife?

STAGE MANAGER: To me it's just a normal place but you people seem to have a problem with it. Some of you call it, the Void. Some of you call it Limbo. I prefer to call it the Green Room.

BOB: I'm in the Void? This is Limbo? I don't want to be in Limbo!

STAGE MANAGER: Who does? It's just something you gotta do, Bob.

BOB: I have things to do. *(He pulls out his diary.)* Look at this appointment book. Full. Do you have any idea how inconvenient this is.

STAGE MANAGER: You're beyond those things, Bob. Relax, enjoy…

BOB: Relax? Enjoy? Enjoy what? There's nothing here. There isn't even a goddamn telephone. Limbo. Jesus Christ! So what am I? A ghost or something?

STAGE MANAGER: I don't know. Metaphysics isn't my thing.

BOB: *(Sudden blinding realization.)* Oh my god! You're god!

   (Falls to his knees.)

STAGE MANAGER: I knew you were going to say that. You all do. And I'll tell you what I tell them … I don't know who this god is, but it's not me.

BOB: I'm in Limbo. I hear a disembodied voice. Who else could you be but god?

STAGE MANAGER: I'm the stage manager.

BOB: What are you talking about?

STAGE MANAGER: Why do I have to go through this everytime one of you shows up here? You're an actor in the play. You had an accident. That's why you're here in the Green Room.

BOB: I'm a business man, not an actor! Here's my card! Bob Crump Enterprises.

STAGE MANAGER: No. You're playing the part of Bob Crump, businessman.

BOB: You're crazy.

STAGE MANAGER: You people are unable to come out of character.

That's a dangerous tendency you know. This is the Green Room. No one is watching you now. Sit down, relax, and forget about your role.

BOB: You said this was Limbo.

STAGE MANAGER: No, no, no, no. You call it Limbo. The void. Purgatory, you name it. We call it the Green Room because that's what it is.

BOB: Listen, isn't there some way I could buy my way out of this?

STAGE MANAGER: That's so Bob Crumpish. I liked your character. I mean I liked the way you played him. He was a real asshole, the kind of creep the audience loves to hate. They'll love the way you went out, too. Just when you seemed to have it all, to get wiped out on the freeway for no reason what-so-ever, whoa … I mean come on, put the audience through some changes why doncha.

BOB: My shattered remains are lying in some hospital and you reduce my life to a role in a soap.

STAGE MANAGER: Hey, so maybe that scene wasn't in your script, but a good actor should know how to improvise.

BOB: What … improvise? I don't improvise.

STAGE MANAGER: Yeah … well maybe you should have thought of that before you tried to drive a car, talk on the phone and light a cigarette at the same time.

BOB: No … it's too cheap … it's too dumb. There has to be more … I don't know … it should mean something. I was an important person. I had money.

STAGE MANAGER: It's plot. What can you do? You can't fight it.

BOB: Plot? I'm a real person … That was a real accident …

STAGE MANAGER: Bob, the world's a stage and you're all players. You know that, Bob.

BOB: This is a sick joke!

STAGE MANAGER: Bob … you played your role and this is the way it worked out.

BOB: This isn't a drama we're dealing with! I'm talking about my life here.

STAGE MANAGER: Bob … you have to accept that this particular story line is over. It was resolved by a sudden, unexpected, random act of violence.

BOB: Goddammit! I've just about had it with this crap.

STAGE MANAGER: If you would stop screaming, we might be able to talk about your options.

BOB: What options?

STAGE MANAGER: I mentioned them earlier but apparently you weren't listening.

BOB: I'm listening now!

STAGE MANAGER: Are you through?

> *(Pause. The STAGE MANAGER waits for BOB to compose himself.)*

If you want, you can relax and hang around the Green Room. There's always the possibility you might get cast in another role.

BOB: Another role? You mean come back as somebody else?

STAGE MANAGER: Or something.

BOB: Something?

STAGE MANAGER: Beggars can't be choosy. You could wind up as a fly or a gorilla. But hey, work is work.

BOB: *(Stands.)* Forget it. I wanna be me. A fly? It's like reincarnation.

STAGE MANAGER: Like what?

BOB: Never mind. You said options. What else?

STAGE MANAGER: If you don't want to be re-cast, there is only one other option.

BOB: So spill it!

STAGE MANAGER: I fade you to black.

BOB: That's it? Oh, great. Just great. So now I'm dead and on top of that there's no afterlife. Isn't that interesting. *(Screaming.)* I want out of here now! Enough is enough!

STAGE MANAGER: What do you want to do, Bob? I can't baby-sit you forever. I've got a show to call.

BOB: This is not happening. I'm me you hear! Me! A somebody! I got money, cars, women …

STAGE MANAGER: Whatever you say. Standby final cue for Bob Crump …

BOB: Final cue?

STAGE MANAGER: Go!

> *(The lights begin a slow fade.)*

BOB: What are you doing?

STAGE MANAGER: Fade to black!

BOB: No! … *(Fading.)* No, please! *(Fading. Weakly, quietly.)* No …
(Blackout. The end.)

The Book of Questions

by Rick Chafe

Characters

ROBERT and SHEILA.

Setting

Their bathroom.

(ROBERT is shaving, SHEILA is sitting on the toilet in a night-gown, drink in hand, reading from a paperback.)

SHEILA: "If you could solve one of the world's problems, but by so doing, none of the others could ever be solved, what would you do?" *(Pause.)* Well?

ROBERT: I don't know.

SHEILA: What do you mean you don't know?

ROBERT: I don't know.

SHEILA: Well, take a guess.

ROBERT: Just one thing?

SHEILA: Just one.

ROBERT: Poverty.

122

SHEILA: Poverty? What about hunger? What about war?

ROBERT: You said one thing. What's wrong with poverty?

SHEILA: So you want everyone to be rich. People won't be any happier if they're rich.

ROBERT: They won't be any happier if they're not hungry either.

SHEILA: Of course they will be. They won't be starving to death.

ROBERT: Well if they aren't poor then they can buy food.

SHEILA: If there's enough food. Or they can just eat their compact discs, and their microwave ovens, and their … Berkenstocks …

ROBERT: Okay, I answered your question.

SHEILA: I just think it's very revealing that you immediately answered that the solution to the world's problems is making everybody rich.

ROBERT: Next question?

SHEILA: Don't you want to hear my answer?

ROBERT: What's your answer.

SHEILA: Egotism.

ROBERT: Fine. Next?

SHEILA: Pick a number.

ROBERT: Forty-three.

(He's now finished shaving, getting his pants on.)

SHEILA: Forty-three … Like a drink?

ROBERT: No thank you.

SHEILA: Get me one?

ROBERT: Of course. I can see you're busy.

(He exits.)

SHEILA: Forty-three … Oh, good one. "An artist friend who has absolutely no talent asks you if you think he has any talent. What do you tell him?" *(Long silence.)* Is that a significant pause?

ROBERT: *(Off.)* He really doesn't have any talent?

SHEILA: Nope.

ROBERT: Then you tell him.

SHEILA: Oh. You'd be perfectly honest?

ROBERT: *(Returning.)* Yeah. He asked. You should tell him. Maybe he does want to know. You have to give people some credit.

(ROBERT hands her a drink.)

SHEILA: Credit. What about people's egos?

ROBERT: *(Checks watch, starts putting on shirt, a little more hurried.)* If I thought his ego was a real big problem, maybe I wouldn't tell him.

SHEILA: So it depends. What if you thought he had some talent, but not nearly as much as he thinks he has?

ROBERT: Sheila, you've got all kinds of talent, I admire your work very much.

SHEILA: Oh, great. This is your friend without any talent?

ROBERT: Shit, this is you, okay? That's what you're asking, isn't it?

SHEILA: No, you don't have any credibility. You just said if you thought I couldn't take it you wouldn't tell the truth.

ROBERT: I'm late.

SHEILA: Chicken shit.

ROBERT: Late chicken shit.

SHEILA: *(Pause.)* I was thinking …

ROBERT: Oh shit.

SHEILA: We've got to talk about some stuff.

ROBERT: Is this going to get heavy?

SHEILA: *I* don't know.

ROBERT: I have to go to work, I have to concentrate all morning, I can't start the day with a heavy conversation, I won't get anything done. Is that enough effort?

SHEILA: Fine. Pick a number.

ROBERT: Nineteen.

SHEILA: Nineteen. Get me a drink?

ROBERT: No.

SHEILA: Nineteen. *(ROBERT'S back is turned. SHEILA puts the book down.)* If you could fall in love with someone, and you knew two things in advance—that it would be wonderful while it lasted, but that he/she would betray you—would you choose to fall in love, or avoid it?

ROBERT: *(Pause.)* So it's a … better to have loved and lost …?

SHEILA: Yeah.

ROBERT: Um. I think … I think pain, is a horrible part of life, but love is … I mean to avoid love is to avoid … What are we living for, anyway?

SHEILA: Love is …?

ROBERT: Love is what we're living for. Or at least something beautiful, to do something good, and worthwhile. Isn't it?

(Pause. He begins to carefully tie his tie.)

SHEILA: I agree.

ROBERT: Mmm.

SHEILA: When you love someone you are giving them the thing they need the most. And to take that away is the worst thing a person can do.

ROBERT: I can see your point. I think that makes a lot of sense.

SHEILA: Betrayal is the worst. I hate lying. Betrayal is much worse than lying. Nothing hurts more.

(Pause. He finishes his necktie.)

Yes, I would go for the love, even if I knew it would end in betrayal. But not a second time.

ROBERT: *(Pause.)* What?

SHEILA: I would not subject myself to the same pain twice. It's not worth it.

ROBERT: If you thought … it was going to happen a second time.

SHEILA: If I knew it was.

ROBERT: How can you know?

SHEILA: You know when there's a pattern of behavior.

ROBERT: What pattern?

SHEILA: I wasn't surprised. I was hurt, but I wasn't surprised. I always knew it was going to happen.

ROBERT: No you didn't.

SHEILA: You were in love with Jan when I met you. You said you were still in love with her but you still wanted to sleep with me.

ROBERT: *(Pause.)* You've been thinking this for three years?

SHEILA: I've always known you would do it again. Eventually. You'll be faithful as long as it's convenient.

ROBERT: Christ. That's very sad.

SHEILA: Yes, it is.

ROBERT: Give me a couple days to get my stuff out.

>*(She nods, exits. He puts on his jacket, straightens his tie and exits. The end.)*

Account Balanced

by Valorie Bunce

Characters

BETTY: A recent widow of sixty some odd years.
LUCILLE: Betty's young married neighbour; a career woman.

Setting

Betty's living room.

BETTY: More tea, dear?

LUCILLE: *(Working on some papers.)* No, no tea. I hate tea.

BETTY: Another sandwich perhaps? Or a dainty? You haven't had any dainties.

LUCILLE: You wouldn't happen to have any instant coffee, would you Betty?

BETTY: Oh no, I'm sorry. We don't drink—I forgot. There is no "we" any more. It's so hard. Sometimes I feel overwhelmed. What will I do without him?

LUCILLE: I don't know. Are these all your T5 slips?

BETTY: I think so. Walter was always the one who filled out the tax returns. I didn't know what to do about them. I kept putting it off.

LUCILLE: It's pretty straight forward, Betty. Especially your return. Nothing too difficult. A few simple calculations—

BETTY: Oh, it's not that I can't do it. I've never been intimidated by mathematics, dear. After all, I've always handled the cheque book. Kept all our accounts balanced. But you see, we each had jobs to do. He had things that he did and I had things that I did. I balanced the accounts. And Walter did the taxes.

LUCILLE: That's alright, Betty. I don't mind. After all, this is what I do best.

BETTY: Oh yes. It certainly is. You're very successful, aren't you? Built yourself quite a career. Traveling all over the place. How exciting it must be. Where was it you were last week?

LUCILLE: Chicago.

BETTY: And before that?

LUCILLE: Ottawa.

BETTY: You're certainly going places, aren't you?

LUCILLE: I have big plans for my future.

BETTY: But—I can't help thinking, dear—it's all a little hard on Brian, isn't it?

LUCILLE: Brian?

BETTY: Yes, your husband, dear.

LUCILLE: I know who he is, Betty. But I disagree with you. It's not hard on him at all. We may have to sacrifice a little time together right now but he's willing to do it. He knows how important my job is to me.

BETTY: Yes, of course. You mustn't mind me. But with his shift work and all … speaking of which, he should be getting home soon, shouldn't he? I can't imagine when the two of you find time to even see each other.

LUCILLE: I wouldn't worry about it, Betty.

BETTY: It's no wonder you haven't started a family yet.

LUCILLE: We aren't going to have a family, Betty.

BETTY: No, no children.

LUCILLE: No. We don't want any.

BETTY: Well, I'm not surprised about you, but I thought Brian …

LUCILLE: I don't know what business it is of yours.

BETTY: Walter and I would've given anything—anything to have had a child.

LUCILLE: You had foster children.

BETTY: Yes, we did.

LUCILLE: Quite a few of them.

BETTY: Twenty-three of them in total. Until the agency decided we were too old.

LUCILLE: Oh, but then you had all the neighbourhood children to play with, didn't you?

BETTY: That reminds me. Have you met our new neighbour?

LUCILLE: The ones across the street? Brian mentioned something about them.

BETTY: I had her over for tea several weeks ago. When you were in, uh, Ottawa was it? She's a nurse you know. Very pretty. Divorced with three young children. But a very nice young lady. Very happy, very bubbly.

LUCILLE: Well, that's nice. I think I'm about done here, Betty.

BETTY: Did I mention I had Brian over to check on the furnace?

LUCILLE: Yes you did. All I have to do now is get a copy of Walter's Last Will and Testament and then I can mail this for you.

(Starts to pack things up.)

BETTY: *(Taking the papers.)* I can do that. *(Pause.)* Did you tell Brian you were going to be here this afternoon?

LUCILLE: I didn't get the chance to.

BETTY: Well, thank you so much, Lucille. It's very good of you to do this for me. Taking time off from work and all. You won't get into any trouble there, will you?

LUCILLE: Of course not. They don't keep tabs on me.

BETTY: So smart. So efficient. That company is so lucky to have you. And I'm lucky to have you as a neighbour.

LUCILLE: I was happy to do it for you. *(She pats BETTY's hand.)*

BETTY: *(Holding on to LUCILLE's hand.)* Oh it's not only this. Look what you did for us when Walter was so ill.

LUCILLE: What do you mean?

BETTY: You were on your holidays those last few weeks in August. Do you remember?

LUCILLE: Of course.

BETTY: Any time I needed to go to the store or the post office or even out for a walk, you were only too happy to come over and sit with my Walter. *(Lets go of LUCILLE's hand.)* I thought at the time you were doing a marvelous thing for me. I really did. And I felt very bad, too, Lucille. Yes, I did. You know as well as I do, that we didn't always see eye-to-eye on things. Well, take for example, our feelings about children.

LUCILLE: Betty, that's all in the past. Let's put the past behind us.

BETTY: I'm not quite sure I'm ready to do that yet. I feel I still have unfinished business to attend to. *(Nervous laugh.)* My accounts aren't balanced, you could say.

LUCILLE: *(Stands.)* Look at the time! Well, I'd love to stay and visit ...

BETTY: Walter and I were together for forty-nine years. Forty-nine years. We loved one another. My Walter. *(LUCILLE sits again.)* Such a sweetheart. It was horrible seeing him die like that. Slowly, bit by bit ...

> *(BETTY starts to cry softly.)*

LUCILLE: Should I call someone to sit with you?

BETTY: How we wanted a child. I don't suppose you can understand that. Two people longing for children of their own. We never could have any. You spend a lot of time fighting the bitterness, the anger. Sure, we took in children, foster children, children who needed us.

LUCILLE: I have to get going, Betty.

> *(Gets up again to leave.)*

BETTY: Nonsense. You can spare some time for a little chat. I want to talk about Walter. Or do you think the people at your work will be angry?

LUCILLE: *(Settling back down.)* Certainly not.

BETTY: Well then, to continue ... After we stopped taking in foster children—

LUCILLE: I know all of this, Betty.

BETTY: We noticed the little children playing in the front street. We invited them all in. "Come, come," Walter would say and he'd bring them into the back yard to the sand box and swing set and the little wooden playhouse he had built so many years before.

LUCILLE: I've heard the story before.

BETTY: I invited the parents over for tea so they could see where their children played. Everyone was happy, Lucille. The children were happy. The parents were happy. Walter was happy.

LUCILLE: Look, Betty, did you forget to take your pills or something?

BETTY: The children were everything to us. They were everything to Walter. Those last days of his when he was still at home, the children were his only source of joy. They knew they were always welcome here. They knew they could come and play whenever they wanted.

LUCILLE: It wasn't right, Betty. He was a sick man.

BETTY: He loved to hear them laugh.

LUCILLE: No person, especially a sick person should have to put up with that kind of noise.

BETTY: Oh surely it couldn't have bothered you that much, Lucille. You never opened your windows all summer long. Surely the sound of your air conditioner was louder than any child's laughter. Surely your pool parties were more raucous than any child playing tag on a hot summer afternoon.

LUCILLE: I never complained. I never said one word—

BETTY: The noise never bothered Walter. Never bothered him at all. It was only when it stopped. *(Pause.)* Only when they stopped coming, when there was nothing but silence that my Walter started dying.

LUCILLE: That's nonsense.

BETTY: *(Accusingly.)* I'm telling you, Lucille, it was the silence that killed him. He refused go outside. He sat here, right here, by this window and watched for them, but they never came back again.

LUCILLE: The man was sick. He was dying. *(Stands and gathers her stuff.)* There was nothing anyone could've done. For your own good, you should stop dwelling on it. Put it behind you. Forget it. He's gone. Whatever happened was for the best.

BETTY: Please. You're right. Don't leave. Stay a moment. You're quite right. For a second I was—caught up in—it's very hard to live without someone. It's very hard. I'm so sorry if I was rude.

LUCILLE: That's all right.

BETTY: I was only trying to sort it out in my head. So that I can forget it. Be finished with it. Put the past behind me.

LUCILLE: As well you should.

BETTY: It's only, I didn't understand why they were afraid …

LUCILLE: Betty—

BETTY: It was the end of August. Remember? You had three weeks off. You were so kind to me then. You would come over and sit with him. Whenever I had to go out, you'd sit with him. And the children. Because they were still coming around then. It was so good of you. I mean, I know you never liked children, but you would still come and stay with him ... and the children. I know what children are like. I can understand you not liking them. So noisy, so messy ...

LUCILLE: Dirty little faces.

BETTY: Their hair never combed.

LUCILLE: Destructive little monsters.

BETTY: *(Checks her watch, looks out the window.)* Yes, they would break things.

LUCILLE: They destroyed your back yard. Traipsed in and out of your house like they owned the place. Trampled your flowers. Absolutely ruined your grass. Screamed and fought the whole time they were here. Why, it's incredible to hear you suggest the little brats were good for Walter. My god—it was the worst thing imaginable. He was a sick person. He should've been in the hospital. But he wasn't. Fine. But to have those filthy little creatures running all over the place. Demanding cookies without so much as a please or thank-you. Sneaking, whispering, whining, plotting god knows what. I put an end to it.

BETTY: Did you?

LUCILLE: I certainly did. I told them the truth. I told them Walter was dying. I told them they should stop coming around.

BETTY: What else? *(Pause.)* What else did you tell the little children, Lucille?

LUCILLE: Nothing—

BETTY: Why, here's Brian home. Such a nice man your husband. And so handsome.

LUCILLE: I really do have to go.

BETTY: Not yet.

LUCILLE: No, I have to.

BETTY: You know, I met the little Johnson boy's mother in the store one day. You remember the Johnson boy. Little red head. Freckles.

LUCILLE: Not really, no. Would you get me my coat please?

BETTY: Of course. It's right here. You must remember the Johnson boy. He used to come every day.

LUCILLE: Well I don't. And I'm tired of talking about it.

BETTY: *(Looking out of the window.)* Oh and here's our new neighbour. Susan. Isn't she lovely? Did I mention I had her over for tea one day?

LUCILLE: Yes you did. Several times. *(She puts on her coat, looks for her gloves.)* I seem to be missing my gloves.

BETTY: As a matter of fact, now that I think about it, it turned out to be the same day Brian was here checking my furnace.

LUCILLE: My gloves?

BETTY: He sat down with us for tea. Yes, now I remember. We had a wonderful time, Lucille. Brian and Susan—that's her name, Susan—they spent the whole afternoon talking and laughing. Oh, they seemed to have so much in common. They talked and talked and then he walked her home.

LUCILLE: What're you talking about?

BETTY: There—there she is. You can see her in her front window. *(LUCILLE looks out the window. Pause.)* Oh, well, Brian must be in there to, uh, help her with her groceries.

> *(BETTY turns away from the window and begins tidying the room. LUCILLE remains transfixed at the window.)*

Now where was I? Oh yes. The Johnson boy. I met his mother in the supermarket. Someone had told the boy he could catch Walter's sickness and die from it. They told him he could catch it just by being here. He could catch it and shrivel up and die. Poor little thing. Mrs. Johnson said he had nightmares for months. Who would tell a child something like that? What kind of mean, spiteful—*(LUCILLE suddenly turns and runs off.)* Why, Lucille—your gloves—*(BETTY looks out the window.)* Dear, dear. People really should be more discrete. *(She continues to tidy.)* If they're going to carry on like that, they should really close the curtains. There now. Everything seems to be in order. Now where did I leave my account books …?

> *(The end.)*

Troth

by William Harrar

Characters

JUDITH and NELSON.

Setting

At first, at Judith and Nelson's separate homes,
later, they are at a party.

---

*(A rumpled, beer-swilling NELSON sits facing stage right. JUDITH
enters stage left, paces, and regards herself in a mirror. She
smokes a cigarette during her speech.)*

JUDITH: It's nine o'clock. The party starts at nine. Of course, we don't
want to be the first ones there, but he's still getting dressed. I think
he's going to wear a suit. *(Looks offstage left.)* Why does he think she
prefers him in a suit? She's an artiste. Surely she would prefer a more
bohemian look. Hey, Peter, lighten up. Don't worry. He didn't hear
that. He's in the bathroom with the radio going full blast. He takes
longer to dress than I do. I've been ready for hours. Because tonight
I'm going to blow her out of the water. See this? *(Indicating her
clothing.)* It's just the sort of Third World-ly stuff she'd wear. Five

134

pound earrings. You know how she dances? Me neither. But I'll find out. A modern dance type, you think? *(Slow, sinuous moves.)* "Look at me, I'm so sensitive, yet so modest about my sensitivity." Oh not that ambitious little ice box. Aerobics, she'll do aerobics, *(Dances aerobically.)* all night … hell, half an hour, if I have to keep this up for half an hour, this flesh is dew. Flash. I'll take pictures. If she can snap low life into high art, so can I. I will document the party for posterity, document her, her and Peter, click click click flash flash and poor Peter will start to wonder why his mistress is so much like his wife, so ordinary, so heavy, stale, useless, *(Exits.)* unprofitable …

> *(NELSON opens a door, stage right and stares off at his wife. He opens his mouth to speak, thinks better of it, and then slouches down in his chair again.)*

NELSON: If she asks me again, I'll say okay. I'm not getting anything done at home. Jesus, it's ten o'clock already. She's not going to ask me again. She's going to say bye and take off, not give me a second thought, probably rejoicing inwardly at how easy it was to ditch the old fart tonight, don't have to listen to his boring complaints all evening. But how do you know? Maybe she really wants me to come to her parties. Maybe she's hurt when I say I can't stand them. I'd like to go up to her and … she's my wife. She's mine. She's so beautiful. I'll hold her and say she's so good-looking, let's stay home tonight. Sure thing. *(Falsetto.)* "Stay home! This party is very important to me." *(Normal voice.)* I guess it must be. Look at that dress she's put on. Almost put on. What she trying to prove? *(Falsetto.)* "My tits haven't sagged as much as yours have." *(Normal voice.)* Damn it, those are my tits. I'll sit home. Wait for her to come back. Maybe vacuum a little. Shit, I'll go to the damn party. I was invited, too. I'll show her I'm … what? I'll show her I'm … a functioning member of society. I'm not a functioning member of society, but I'll show her I can pretend. *(Rehearsing his announcement.)* "Incidentally, I'm coming with you to the party. I think there might be some people there who can help me find work. Perhaps your friend, Peter the Bureaucrat … " Jesus, I hope nobody knows I've been canned …

> *(At the party. JUDITH enters, snapping pictures. She takes a picture of a couple—actually her husband, Peter, and NELSON's wife, Margo—waves and laughs. To NELSON:)*

JUDITH: Smile. C'mon, smile. Okay, don't. The camera wants only the truth.

(She thrusts the camera in his face. He knocks it out of her hands with his beer bottle. JUDITH looks at the camera on the floor and then at NELSON. She kicks the camera away.)

Is that your wife?

NELSON: Excuse me?

JUDITH: Is that your wife—dancing? Margo?

NELSON: Yes. With your husband?

JUDITH: Yes. You must be Nelson.

NELSON: I must be.

JUDITH: I'm Judith Solsgirth. I think you know my husband.

NELSON: Peter. The deputy ... um ...

JUDITH: Assistant Deputy Minister.

NELSON: Still in Corrections?

JUDITH: Yes.

NELSON: What impresses me is how well he dresses. I'd be embarrassed to spend so much on decorating myself, but he carries it off quite well.

(JUDITH studies NELSON's clothing disapprovingly.)

It's all I can do to put on a tie anymore.

JUDITH: Isn't your wife a fashion photographer?

NELSON: A photographer. News. Originally. I got her a job with the Free Press. She's branching out. In fact she's going to have her own show downtown next month. Portraits of prisoners. Side by side with their mug shots.

JUDITH: Ah, that's where Peter comes in. He got her permission to visit Stony Mountain.

NELSON: In March.

JUDITH: Since March. I remember. At the end of March he went skiing.

(NELSON is momentarily startled.)

Do you ski?

NELSON: No.

JUDITH: Your wife?

NELSON: Yes, as a matter of fact, she's quite keen. Gets together with her buddies and takes off for a long weekend.

JUDITH: You're a reporter.

NELSON: Yeah, I ...

JUDITH: Didn't you write a series on prison reform last year? After the riots?

NELSON: Yes. A three-part.

JUDITH: You called my husband ignorant. You said he was in over his head.

NELSON: No, no. I simply reported that informed opinion held that he didn't—

JUDITH: He hasn't forgotten. *(She watches her husband dance.)* Planning a sequel?

NELSON: I'm kind of freelance now.

JUDITH: Oh ... I'm studying photography. Hoping to get a few pointers from your wife. When she has a minute. Another drink?

NELSON: What time is it?

JUDITH: Eleven.

NELSON: I think I'll go home. I shouldn't have come. I've forgotten why people like parties.

JUDITH: Please stay. Why don't you ask me to dance?

NELSON: I'm not much of a dancer.

JUDITH: That's not stopping anyone else.

NELSON: I don't feel I can do it.

JUDITH: Please. Just for a bit.

> *(They dance silently for a moment.)*

NELSON: You dance like my wife.

JUDITH: Thank you.

NELSON: It wasn't a compliment.

> *(He looks around for his wife.)*

JUDITH: Perhaps they've gone ... oh, let me see ... admiring the garden, though Peter doesn't know flowers from floor mops, but your wife— has she a green thumb?

NELSON: *(Long pause.)* Are you sure?

JUDITH: Aren't you?

NELSON: She hasn't said anything.

JUDITH: Keep dancing.

NELSON: She would tell me, wouldn't she? How do you know about it?

JUDITH: We've agreed to let each other know.

NELSON: How thoughtful. Can't you keep your husband to yourself. Can't you please him?

JUDITH: He goes where he's welcomed. Aren't we dancing? I wouldn't be terribly concerned about your wife. I think she's only paying off a debt to Peter. As soon as she has her opening … Although … has your wife said anything about a trip in August?

(NELSON looks at her, alarmed.)

Peter's taking a month long seminar …

NELSON: She's going to Montreal.

JUDITH: … at McGill.

NELSON: I want her to know I know.

JUDITH: You're going to make it worse.

NELSON: It can't get worse, you blind idiot.

JUDITH: Me? Blind?

(NELSON walks about searching for his wife, opening doors, nodding at other party goers. He opens a door and steps outside.)

Still some light.

NELSON: Can't be. It's midnight.

JUDITH: But it's the longest day of the year. First day of summer.

NELSON: The days are getting shorter. *(Slaps himself.)* Damn bugs.

JUDITH: Is that a firefly?

NELSON: They make a lot of noise.

JUDITH: It's a warm night.

NELSON: They got to crowd their whole year—their whole life—into one night. I had to resign from the newspaper. I copied somebody else's story. I haven't been able to work. It was me who taught her everything she knows. Then she gets this prisoner idea. It's so phony. I bet they're going at it in the back of this van.

JUDITH: *(Quietly.)* No, they're not.

NELSON: Watch this. The earth will move.

(He jumps up and down on the van's front fender.)

JUDITH: They're not in there. Peter has to have it just so.

NELSON: That's when he's with you. When he's with someone he loves, he'll do it in the road.

(JUDITH tries to slap NELSON but he stops her.)

Why is he younger than you?

JUDITH: He's not, chronologically. He doesn't age. I do. So tell me, what kind of a camera does Margo own? Does she use a tripod? How does she take pictures? Is she impulsive? Does she arrange everything beforehand?

NELSON: She just fires away. She wastes a fortune on film.

JUDITH: Is that how she makes love?

NELSON: I wouldn't know. Ask your husband.

JUDITH: When you first met her, how did you kiss? When you were first married, how did you …

NELSON: I could touch her and just tell if she wanted to.

JUDITH: Did you undress before you went to bed?

NELSON: Bed?

JUDITH: Oh. When you … Is she serious? Does she smile?

NELSON: Serious.

JUDITH: Close her eyes?

NELSON: Yes. She concentrates.

JUDITH: On herself or on you?

NELSON: On herself. God, I didn't need any help.

JUDITH: Did she make any unusual noises?

NELSON: No. I took it to mean she was honest. Silly me.

JUDITH: How does she hold you?

NELSON: She doesn't.

JUDITH: How *did* she? What part of her body does she want you to feel?

NELSON: She knew I liked her breasts.

JUDITH: They're not that big, are they?

NELSON: When she's undressing she lets them out for moment and they look at me—two sad eyes begging me for comfort. But she won't let me. She hides them away.

(JUDITH presses against NELSON. He steps away from her.)

Get serious, will ya.

JUDITH: Why? Why?

NELSON: *(Backs away.)* I'm sorry. I can't. I'm too afraid.

JUDITH: Of me?

NELSON: Of my life. What's left of it.

JUDITH: I'll get out of here.

NELSON: Why don't you divorce him? You've got the dough.

JUDITH: Oh sure, fuck off, Peter. Ha ha. He wouldn't believe it. Do your kids know?

NELSON: I don't think so.

JUDITH: My kids were the ones who told me. This was years ago. I asked Jennifer who her best friend was. Then she asked me. "Daddy," I said. *(Raises her voice to become a little girl's voice.)* "Daddy's best friend is Miss Bambridge." *(She turns away, breaks down.)* Miss Bambridge. Her grade two teacher.

NELSON: *(Touching her shoulder.)* Leave the bum.

JUDITH: *(Leaning into him.)* I couldn't face my parents. He's the only thing I've accomplished.

NELSON: Oops. There they are.

> *(NELSON pulls away from JUDITH.)*

JUDITH: Where?

NELSON: Coming out of those trees.

JUDITH: A blanket under his arm. Boy, he's going to be itchy tomorrow. Everywhere.

NELSON: They're coming this way.

JUDITH: No, they're not.

NELSON: Yes, they are. She waved. They've seen us.

JUDITH: What are you going to say?

NELSON: I don't know. I don't know.

> *(JUDITH takes his hand.)*

What are you doing?

JUDITH: Just ... help me.

NELSON: *(Pause.)* Judith?

JUDITH: What?

NELSON: Margo, me and Margo, we used to kiss like this.

> *(They kiss. The end.)*

Love and Ladybugs

by Lora Schroeder and Tannis Kowalchuk

Characters

A MAN in his fifties and a WOMAN in her forties.

Setting

A bare stage with two window frames, large enough for a person to walk through, suspended on either side of the stage. Stage right is the MAN's playing space. He also has a plant sitting on a small table and a plain wooden kitchen chair just upstage right of his window. Stage left is the WOMAN's playing space. An identical chair is placed upstage left of her window. A bowl sits under her chair.

MAN: *(To ladybug in his hand.)* Yup. There were twenty-four of you. Right in a row, marching off to do your duty. Of course, it's not really a duty. Makes it more interesting, though, to imagine it as a duty. Duty, hah!

WOMAN: *(Putting on her boots.)* C'mon girl, don't dawdle. It's good picking this year, that's for sure. My god, I was out there just last week and I picked two pails worth of berries the size of eyeballs. Huge suckers! And I know exactly where they are.

(She steps through the window frame.)

141

MAN: People are always talking about your duty. Telling you what they think ... telling you what to do. Telling you, "You ain't happy," but they know how to fix that. Telling me I ain't happy.

WOMAN: Damn these boots. *(She bends to adjust them.)*

MAN: *(Looking out the window.)* Quit looking at me funny! Don't come on my yard. Don't come on my yard if you're gonna look at me funny!

WOMAN: *(Begins to walk, staring at berries on the ground.)* This is alright. Blueberries right in your own backyard practically. Not too bad. *(Looks closer.)* No, already been picked over.

MAN: *(To ladybug.)* Funny. Funny. Funny how you things fly. You'd never know it, to look at you, that you could fly. Look too round I'd say, and hard. Now a bird, it's got soft wings ... well, soft looking. Course you can't bend their feathers neither ... they'd just snap.

WOMAN: No bears to give me any trouble either. If I ever saw one, I'd swallow my tongue and pass right out in front of it. And he'd get a good meal out of the deal too. I'm still pretty tender. Ah geez! These boots are frigged. *(Adjusts them again.)* Okay. I know where there's a good patch. *(Moving further to centre stage.)*

MAN: *(To ladybug.)* But you m'lady, you've got round, hard half-moons for wings ... that crunch.

WOMAN: Now, I can't lose track of the time.

MAN: *(To window.)* Telling me I ain't happy.

WOMAN: I gotta get back to the house soon and give Mom a hand with all those damn beets. Canning beets. I hate that goddamn work, staining up your hands pink for days and days—sweet Jesus, my god, these are rocks, not berries. Start shoveling.

(She crouches and picks berries.)

MAN: *(To bug.)* You're the last one. Last of the twenty-four. Others have all disappeared. Swallowed up in this old place. Maybe they went back out there. *(To window.)* Back to their own yard. But you'll pull her through, eh ... eat up all those nasties.

WOMAN: *(Picking.)* Psych ... psych-ol-ogy. Psychology. Interesting stuff there. All that jazz about your dreams and what it means if a cow starts talking to you or you friend dies. It's interesting, all those articles in the Chatelaine prescription Mom's got. It's important to keep up with what's going on. It sure as hell doesn't hurt. But the problem section's got to be the best. "Dear so and so, my husband is having an affair with my best friend. What should I do?" *(Inhales a whistle.)* Some people sure have trouble. That's for sure.

MAN: There you go. *(Setting the ladybug by the plant.)* No. Off this way.

(He tries to direct the bug to the plant)

No. Don't fly away!

(He crushes it.)

WOMAN: If you're thinking about something really hard, or at night time, or if you keep dreaming about the same thing over and over ... like a man for example, if you can actually picture something happening so perfectly, and play that picture over and over in your head, I think it could actually happen to you.

MAN: Mama always said, "If you've got ladybugs, your plants will thrive." *(He grabs a jar.)* Catching them is one thing, it's keeping them that makes for trouble. *(He stands by the window.)* They're just sitting out there, sunning their backs, waiting.

WOMAN: It could actually happen to you. That's what I think.

(MAN steps through the window.)

MAN: Oh, hello.

WOMAN: Oh, Jesus Christ!

MAN: Sorry. Didn't mean to startle you.

WOMAN: Now where did you come from?

MAN: Guess the dampness muffled the sound.

(Pause.)

WOMAN: Pardon?

MAN: Guess the dampness muffled the sound.

WOMAN: Oh.

MAN: Well.

(Pause.)

WOMAN and MAN: *(Together.)* Doing some picking?

WOMAN: Berries.

MAN: Bugs.

(WOMAN inhales another whistle.)

Ladybugs ... for the aphids ... if you've got ladybugs, your plants will thrive ... they eat up all the aphids.

(Pause.)

WOMAN: Well, nice enough day we're having.

MAN: Yup. Sure is. *(Pause.)* Didn't expect to find anyone this far back.

WOMAN: Oh, I guess I wandered over a bit too far. I was looking for a good patch to park myself.

MAN: It's alright. Mama never had much use for the berries. Didn't mind if other people did their picking here. Guess I don't either.

WOMAN: Yes, I heard about her passing on. Must have been hard on you. *(Looks at pail.)* I'll be able to make a nice pie out of this, maybe two. All alone now?

MAN: Yup.

WOMAN: *(Breathing in.)* Yup.

> *(They both freeze, take two steps back, turn and go back through their own windows and sit on their chairs. WOMAN takes a handful of berries from her pail, squishes them in her hand and puts the mush in a bowl. She repeats this action throughout the following.)*

He's not bad looking. Just a little overweight here and there. And his eyes are kind of strange. Remind me of pig's eyes. But that's alright. You can't have everything. He's probably very nice. It's the real handsome ones who are the bastards, and I sure as hell don't want to end up crying into my pillow and sending letters to bloody Chatelaine's magazine. But that fellow seemed really nice. *(Pause.)* I could have asked him out to see a movie or something. I was going to! Christ, he would have said yes, I'm sure. What has he got to lose? *(Pause.)* Well, it's not like I'm not going to see him ever again. We're neighbours, practically.

MAN: People always interfering. Telling me what to do, "Got to get yourself a woman." Been here eight years, since Mama died, without one. Never had a real one, a wife that is. What I want one now for? *(To plant.)* Hey, my beauty?

WOMAN: Who knows, he might just come around here tomorrow to borrow some milk, or god knows what. Like they do on TV. And I'll just say, "Hi. How about seeing a movie one night?" Or something like that. Jeannie Douglas would lend me one of her fancy numbers, and I'd just go. He's not bad looking.

MAN: *(Picking up a dead ladybug.)* Now, I'm not one of those that goes around stomping on things just cause they're crawling where they ain't got no business to be crawling. Why are you always trying to get away? Shouldn't try to control what you can't control. What's an old bugger need company for anyway? Funny looking wings.

WOMAN: Okay, Mom. Berries are ready.

MAN: But you fly all right.

(Blackout. The end.)

Razed by Wolves

by Phil McBurney

Characters

NORMAN: Aged forty-nine, but older than his years. He is serene and relaxed—looking more like a friendly grampa than a former wife abuser.

JJ: Aged twenty-four. Norman's estranged son. A member of an up-and-coming rock group, he wears long hair tied in a ponytail, fingerless gloves, a long overcoat, jeans and high-top runners.

ELSIE: About the same age as Norman; his current wife.

Setting

A screen door is set on a large riser, centre stage, at an angle to the audience. The riser represents the interior of a small bungalow in a working class area of Vancouver.

(Inside the house, NORMAN sits in an easy chair reading a book and listening to classical music. Enter JJ. He carries a small piece of paper and checks the house number above the screen door against the information on the paper. JJ's actions are tentative: he is almost feeling his way along, at odds with himself and ready to bolt. He enters the yard through an imaginary gate and climbs the

146

sidewalk towards the screen door. As he climbs, he notices the elaborate flowers along the sidewalk. Finally, he gathers himself and knocks, gingerly at first and then, angry at his own reticence, more aggressively.)

NORMAN: *(Puts down his book.)* Just a minute. *(Then in a more jolly manner as he stands up with difficulty and walks towards the door with an arthritic limp.)* Just a minute. I don't get around like I used to. *(Approaches the door.)* Yes? Are you selling something?

JJ: *(Speechless for a second.)* Uh, no.

NORMAN: It's okay. I'm not rude to salesmen. Sold vacuum cleaners once myself. Desperate. You selling vacuum cleaners?

JJ: I, uh—

NORMAN: Magazines? I can't afford magazines. Had a young guy a while ago—tattoos up and down his arms—said he was working his way through college selling magazines. Like hell. But, like I said, can't afford them.

JJ: I, uh, I think I have the wrong address. Sorry. I've disturbed you.

(Stands speechless for a moment, looking NORMAN in the face, then turns and walks back toward the street.)

NORMAN: *(Opens the door to speak, calls out.)* You're John, aren't you?

JJ: *(Stops in mid-stride, blurts out as if caught in some act of stealth.)* Yes. *(Then with some anger as he turns away.)* Yes, I'm John.

(Pause.)

NORMAN: *(Steps outside, and speaks in a sudden confessional tone.)* I been sober seven years now.

(JJ's body language shows he's ready to explode any minute. NORMAN faces JJ.)

I don't blame you.

JJ: No?

NORMAN: If you hate me, I mean.

JJ: Oh, I hate you, all right. No problem there.

NORMAN: You got good reason. Good reason.

JJ: You broke her nose. I watched you.

(Pause.)

NORMAN: But I turned myself around. A bit, I did. And I'm sorry for what I did—

JJ: Oh, you were always sorry.

NORMAN: Not, I guess, that it matters now ... son.

JJ: No, it didn't matter to you then and it doesn't matter to me now.

NORMAN: *(Giving in evidence.)* Look. These flowers. I planted them myself.

JJ: Flowers, shit. I don't care about any flowers.

   (He is still unable to act on his anger. Pause.)

NORMAN: You look like a fine boy, John. Not such a boy anymore, either. *(Pause.)* I—I did love her once, your mother. You know, before the alcohol.

JJ: You don't seem to understand. I came here to lay a beating on you, man, you know that?

NORMAN: I'm not blaming that. The alcohol, I mean. I can't stand it when people use that to excuse the bad things they do. I was a—I was a terrible person.

JJ: Son of a bitch!

NORMAN: Yes, a son of a bitch, if you like. Now I ... I pull weeds and prune shrubs. Things can happen in a person's life—God?—you know, to bring us to our knees. *(Pause.)* Ah, look, I talk too much.

JJ: *(Relents a little.)* I came here to lay a beating on you. Joannie told me not to. *(Pause.)* Joannie's fine. She's starting college in September.

NORMAN: College? *(Pleased.)* That's something. She was a smart little thing right from day one.

JJ: How would you know? You were never there, and when you were, you were either drunk or hung over.

NORMAN: Well, I won't deny that. *(Pause.)* And you? What do you do?

JJ: I play—*(Then realises what he's said.)* I stock shelves actually. And I play in a band.

NORMAN: Band?

JJ: Razed by Wolves. Maybe you heard—naw. Not likely. We're recording, making a tape. That's why we're in Vancouver.

NORMAN: Well, that's good. I played guitar once.

JJ: *(Interested, in spite of his anger.)* You did?

NORMAN: Before you were born. I traded it for a case of beer one night.

JJ: *(Disgusted and disappointmented.)* A case of beer.

NORMAN: My life for a case of beer. *(Pause.)* You drink?

JJ: No.

NORMAN: Good. That's good. I read somewhere about kids of alcoholics. I'd hate to think—

JJ: I mean I had a few when I was fifteen. Never got a taste for it. Mom's dead against it.

NORMAN: Your mother, uh, Myrna's a trooper. She sets her mind to something, nothing changes it. Spunk. I guess that's what attracted me to her in the first place. Did she—did she re-marry?

JJ: No. One jerk a lifetime was enough, she said. She's happy. Smokes too much maybe.

NORMAN: About the beating, I guess I can't blame you for that.

JJ: You aren't what I expected. Big. I remember you towering over me. Hands with huge fingers. *(NORMAN looks at his hands which he holds limply in front of him.)* Calluses. *(Pause.)* But you're not what I expected.

ELSIE: *(Off.)* Norman.

NORMAN: My wife. Elsie. She, well, we live together. We met at an A.A. meeting, actually. She'd like to meet you. I can't remember if—

JJ: Anyway. I gotta go. I—I'm glad I saw you. I think so. It's over now.

NORMAN: Over?

JJ: The anger. It's gone. I think so. Can't …

NORMAN: Well, that's good. Should we shake hands then?

    (Long pause.)

JJ: Naw. Let's just leave it like this.

NORMAN: Tell her—tell Myrna—*(Pause.)* No good. Tell her nothing.

ELSIE: *(Off.)* Norman, you outside, honey?

NORMAN: Good-bye, son.

    (They part. NORMAN turns and re-enters his house. JJ waves awkwardly after him, watching his father's back. Slowly he turns and walks away, checking over his shoulder. He exits. ELSIE enters.)

ELSIE: Who was that? Salesman?

NORMAN: Nice young man.

ELSIE: Oh?

NORMAN: Selling magazine subscriptions or something. From Winnipeg, actually.

ELSIE: *(Fussing about the room.)* Winnipeg. You ever think about Winnipeg? Ever want to go back? See your family?

NORMAN: Nope. I burned those bridges. Or they were burned for me. I doubt if I'd even know my own kids if I saw them on the street. No, I know I wouldn't.

ELSIE: I wonder if people ever get those magazines. Crooks.

NORMAN: *(Taking up his book again.)* Well, this fellow seemed honest. Probably has a great future. Listen, your daughter ever mention a rock band called Razed by Wolves?

ELSIE: No. Megadeth. Guns 'n Roses. No Razed by Wolves. Why? What made you think of that?

NORMAN: Oh nothing really. Just something that fella said.

ELSIE: Oh, you want tea? Water should be boiling by now.

   (Exits. Pause.)

NORMAN: *(Unaware that she's gone.)* Sure. Ever wish you could do it over again? Re-live your life. Undo all the damage. Pour all the booze back in the bottle. Elsie?

   (He realizes she's not there, shrugs. He looks at his book again, then puts it down. He moves to the stereo set and fumbles aimlessly through the FM channels until he hits a station that's tolerable, playing the Mike and the Mechanics' song, "The Living Years." As the music plays, he goes to the screen door and looks out, hoping for one last glimpse of his son. The end.)

Learning to Drive

by Ellen Peterson

Characters

A STUDENT, over sixteen, and
a TEACHER, a driving instructor of any age.

Setting

A bare stage.

(The light comes up on the STUDENT. The TEACHER is in darkness when not in the scene.)

STUDENT: In the beginning of the Year of Not Pretending I woke up crying and thought: You might as well be happy. There is no time to waste. Just before the beginning of the Year of Not Pretending I learned to drive. I felt it was time. The teacher I found through the yellow pages was heavy and had tired eyes for a young man. He had obviously watched too much hockey.

(A light comes up on the TEACHER, seated on a mat. He strikes a gong.)

TEACHER: Lessons are thirty-five dollars for an hour and a half. I've never taught anyone who needed more than five lessons. I'm a good teacher. I'll tell you what you need to pass the test but I'll also teach you to drive. I'm going to ask you to do things that are illegal to see if you're listening. I like it when people ask questions. Got any?

STUDENT: No.

TEACHER: Okay. There are two pedals, but we use only one foot. The gas is the one on the right. The other is the brake. Can you reach?

STUDENT: Yes.

TEACHER: Adjust the rear-view mirror so you can see as much out the rear window as possible. Start the car.

STUDENT: You mean you want me to drive this thing right now?

TEACHER: What else? Put your foot on the brake, put the car in drive, and pull out onto Main Street.

STUDENT: You're out of your mind.

(Sound of gong, lights out on TEACHER.)

It was rush hour. Nobody got hurt. I came home and drank three beers. During the second lesson I was much calmer.

(Lights come up on TEACHER.)

TEACHER: Change lanes to the left.

STUDENT: Oh lord.

TEACHER: Signal your intention. Rear-view mirror. And shoulder check.

STUDENT: Signalmirrorshouldercheck. God.

TEACHER: That's when you're supposed to actually change lanes. Well don't just stop.

STUDENT: Oh.

TEACHER: Why did you stop?

STUDENT: I don't know.

TEACHER: Well don't stop in the middle of traffic.

STUDENT: Okay.

TEACHER: Try again. Signal. Mirror.

STUDENT: Signalmirrorshouldercheck.

TEACHER: Don't stop. Why do you stop?

STUDENT: I wasn't sure … There was too much to do all at once! I'll never learn this.

TEACHER: Sure you will.

(Sound of gong, lights out on TEACHER.)

STUDENT: I pretended that I was all right. That I didn't mind having to go through this. That this hideous feeling of incompetence didn't bother me. I tried to appear eager, and pleased to be gaining a new and useful skill. There's a good reason why most people learn to drive when they're sixteen. When you're sixteen you don't know you can die. If you're much older than that, not only do you know you're going to die, you also know that this is probably where. Lesson three. I approached the third lesson confidently. Nothing much to this driving thing, really. I am a smart, competent person. Lots of people who are much more stupid than me can drive; I can certainly learn to drive. I was feeling cocky and expansive. My teacher and I chatted. *(Lights up on TEACHER.)* Do you like teaching?

TEACHER: I guess.

STUDENT: Then it happened. Someone slammed on the brake. Somehow I don't think it was me.

TEACHER: Didn't you see that?

STUDENT: What? What!?

TEACHER: You didn't see it. Keep your eyes on the road. Don't stop! Why did you stop?

STUDENT: I don't know. Out of the corner of my eye I could see the teacher shaking his head. What had I done? I suppose this was when it came home to me that what I had to learn was potentially deadly, and I had better pay attention. For the next lesson, I decided that my problem was that I was too tense and if I could just relax the whole thing would come naturally. I babbled. I made stupid jokes and counted to three in a different language at each stop sign. I blathered on about the psychology of learning. I realize now that I was, of course, trying to sound smart because he knew how to drive and I didn't. *(To TEACHER.)* You know, I think the problem with driving is that all of a sudden you're, like, two thousand pounds heavier, and what I think you have to do is you have to sort of re-learn the boundaries of where you end, you know?

TEACHER: And watch out for that pedestrian.

STUDENT: Do you find that you have to teach each student differently? I mean, does each student have different things that they understand, or different ways that they learn?

TEACHER: I guess.

STUDENT: Do you ever fear for your life?

TEACHER: There's been a few students who've tried to kill me. The really dangerous ones are the ones who think that they already know how.

STUDENT: I'm glad I don't have that problem.

TEACHER: And the ones who don't pay attention.

STUDENT: Oh. I kind of thought I was getting the hang of it. In the fifth and hopefully final lesson we worked on the details; the difference between simply operating a motorized vehicle, and being able to pull it off on the test.

(The sound of a gong.)

TEACHER: Watch out for that pedestrian and don't stop when you make a mistake.

STUDENT: And of course, this lesson was my first glimpse into the mysteries of parallel parking.

TEACHER: You must pump the brake three times when preparing to parallel park, grasshopper.

STUDENT: Is that magic, for good luck?

TEACHER: Whatever. Then move forward until you are lined up with the car in front, this pole. Turn the wheel and back up until you have pole number three right in the middle of your driver's side mirror, turn the wheel the other way and just ease right in.

STUDENT: Perfect. Easy. A dream. Then suddenly, a premonition. It's not going to be like this in the real world, is it? I mean, the poles are never going to be the right distance apart, are they?

TEACHER: No. But you might drive all your life and never have to parallel park again.

(Gong.)

STUDENT: As we drove to the test, my teacher blessed me with all the wisdom that remained.

TEACHER: Whatever you do, keep your eyes open and don't stop when you make a mistake. Also, remember to signal. Signalling your intentions is good. If you go even one kilometer over the limit you'll fail. If any part of your car is over the stop line you'll fail. If you fail to yield the right-of way to a vehicle entering traffic from an uncontrolled intersection, you'll fail.

STUDENT: Tough world out there.

TEACHER: You don't even know. If he doesn't like you, you'll fail. They have quotas. They have to fail a certain number of people, even if they don't have a reason.

STUDENT: Do you think I'll pass?

TEACHER: How should I know? But what you should do is talk like you do. Be your entertaining self. It'll help you relax, and it can't hurt.

(Gong, lights down on the TEACHER.)

STUDENT: I was never sure what he thought of me. I could never tell if he meant it when he said I'd be fine or I was doing well, because of how awful he made me feel when I did something careless. He just left it all up to me.

(Gong.)

I was very charming and drove well and passed the test. I was kind of sorry to say good-bye to the teacher—despite the tension and how I hated at first to pay someone to scrutinize my every move, it had turned out to be kind of fun.

(Lights up.)

TEACHER: Good-bye. Drive carefully.

(Lights down.)

STUDENT: Suddenly there you are. The powers that be have told you you can go ahead. You have the required skills. Freedom! And you realize with painful clarity that you are alone, you are in control of a powerful machine, and you do not know how to drive. The powers that be know nothing. There is only one brake and you're the only one that can use it. You must make all the decisions. Is it now safe to make this left-hand turn? There is no one to remind you about speeding and its dire consequences. No sign on the top of the car that says: "New at this. Thank you for getting out of the way." And there, suddenly, you are. This is lesson six. Time passes and I'm not dead yet. Although driving in traffic still causes a certain amount of indigestion, what I now love is to take my little car very late at night or early in the morning and just drive when no one knows I'm gone. I wonder if other people do this? What I do not like is driving with passengers in the car.

(Lights up on the TEACHER. He is white-knuckled, petrified.)

Scared yet?

TEACHER: *(Through clenched teeth.)* Oh no, you're doing fine.

STUDENT: I may be imagining this.

(Lights down on TEACHER.)

It's just that I am scarcely comfortable taking responsibility for my own life in this way. I can't say I'm ready to risk someone else's life, limb, or peace of mind. But it can be necessary, depending on where you're going. And it's nice, after all these years of depending on others to take me places, to be one of those people who can pick somebody up at the airport, or to say at the end of the night: Does anyone need a ride?

(The TEACHER holds up a sign which reads "No thanks!" and the audience shouts back "No thanks!")

I may be imagining this.

(Gong.)

It's fun to come and go as I please. One morning, early, I decide I need a holiday, and look at the map and drive to a place-name I like the sound of. It is a very nice little town in the hills but there isn't anything there to stay for. But getting there was fun. And on leaving town I think the crossroad looks considerably more interesting than the highway. I think of Robert Frost. It is beautiful. Hills, and other unexpected things. Smoky looking trees, and creeks, and farms at the bend in the road. My heart sings. I drive and drive. I turn corners on whims. I am trying to remember the poem ... "and sorry I could not travel both / And be one traveler ..." when I round a fated bend and am in the ditch before I know. Nothing to be done. I am oddly not in the least upset. The nearest farm is close. The door is opened by a kid of about nineteen, with tired eyes, who has obviously watched too much hockey.

(Lights up.)

TEACHER: Stuck in the ditch?

STUDENT: Pretty much. He can't push me out as the car is up to the windows in snow. So he calls the farmer from up the road, who has been drinking and looks sad. He comes with his truck, hooks the chain to my car, and somehow my car appears to pull his truck into the ditch. I didn't notice the ice. His wife comes with the tractor and they pull first the truck and then me out of the ditch. Thank you so much. Thanks a lot. Can I pay you for your trouble?

TEACHER: If you see someone in the ditch someday, help them out. Drive carefully.

(Gong and lights down on the TEACHER.)

STUDENT: It is New Year's Eve. So in the beginning of the Year of Not Pretending I learned to drive. I try to enjoy the road. Sometimes I even parallel park. So much traffic. All doing the same things every day; never learning and continuing to live. I find that almost no one signals their intentions or comes to a full and complete stop. We pay little attention to each other. We feel we must be moving and we are not. Sitting still while the vehicles move, we are in a dangerous situation and we must learn again and again and again that Robert Frost was right. And for some reason that is shrouded in the mists of wisdom, elderly men in hats are extremely dangerous behind the wheel. You can't tell if they know you're there. People should have to take refresher courses.

(Gong. The end.)

Accidental Death of a Salesman

by Nick Mitchell

Characters

ARTHUR: Arthur Miller, the playwright.
WILLY: A businessman.
WAITRESS ONE and WAITRESS TWO.

Setting

A restaurant.

(WAITRESS ONE shows ARTHUR to his table. She gives the table a wipe, and shakes her head. WAITRESS TWO is hiding behind a post, watching. She is highly offended by WAITRESS ONE's criticism.)

WAITRESS ONE: The part-time help they hire these days! *(Pause.)* There you go, Mr. Miller! Spotless! Your usual?

ARTHUR: Please!

(As soon as WAITRESS ONE exits, WAITRESS TWO approaches with a towel over her arm. ARTHUR has taken his script out of an envelope, and is looking it over.)

WAITRESS TWO: *(Clearing her throat.)* Ahem!

ARTHUR: Yes? *(Looks up.)* I'm already looked after.

WAITRESS TWO: The gentleman at table two was wondering if he might join you?

ARTHUR: Table two?

WAITRESS TWO: If you look down that aisle, towards the window. Past the thin blonde sitting with the bald fat man. Ah! There he is! He's the one who's waving.

ARTHUR: *(Squinting.)* I don't know him. Really, I don't have the time.

WAITRESS TWO: If I might be so bold; it might be worth your while.

ARTHUR: I don't think so.

WAITRESS TWO: *(Not listening.)* I'll just bring him over.

> *(She leaves.)*

ARTHUR: Please, I'm busy with something!

> *(WAITRESS TWO returns with WILLY.)*

WILLY: I'm so glad you agreed to see me, Mr. Miller.

ARTHUR: But I didn't! I was just telling the waitress here …

> *(WILLY sits down as WAITRESS TWO pulls his chair back for him.)*

WILLY: Can I call you Arthur?

ARTHUR: No, you cannot!

WILLY: Even better! I'll just call you Art.

> *(WAITRESS ONE returns with a drink.)*

WAITRESS ONE: *(To WAITRESS TWO.)* This is my table!

WAITRESS TWO: *(Putting a hand on WILLY's shoulder.)* I'm with him!

ARTHUR: *(Stern.)* I just want to be left alone.

> *(WAITRESS ONE looks sternly at WAITRESS TWO.)*

WILLY: *(Playing on guilt.)* Surely, you'll at least hear me out!

> *(WAITRESS TWO gives WAITRESS ONE a look of appeal.)*

ARTHUR: *(Giving up.)* Oiii …

> *(WAITRESS ONE gives in with a sigh.)*

WAITRESS TWO: *(To WILLY.)* Can I get you something?

WILLY: Is that gin and tonic? I'll have the same.

> *(While WAITRESS TWO and WILLY discuss his drink, WAITRESS ONE leans over to ARTHUR so only he can hear.)*

WAITRESS ONE: Let's not make a scene. Leave it to me, Mr. Miller. I'll get rid of him.

WAITRESS TWO: With lemon?

(WILLY gives WAITRESS TWO a pinch on the bum.)

WILLY: Just a squeeze.

(WAITRESS TWO leaves and WAITRESS ONE follows, giving ARTHUR a knowing wink.)

(To ARTHUR.) Let's get to the point, Art!

(WILLY brings a manuscript out of an envelope. ARTHUR reads the title upside down. He is startled.)

You're wondering how I got my hands on this. I can't reveal my sources. And it really doesn't matter! The point is that I like it! Love it! And I want to make you an offer.

ARTHUR: But I can't!

WILLY: Yes, you can! That's what I'm here to tell you. We'll buy out your producers. Money is no object!

ARTHUR: *(Possibly thinking of clauses in his contract.)* Oh, I don't know ...

WILLY: It's brilliant of course! I liked it so much! Maybe because my name is Willy too. Its a work of genius! No matter what the name!

ARTHUR: *(Modestly.)* Well ... thanks.

WILLY: That was me! My story! That's why I'm prepared to go to such lengths. Absolutely brilliant!

ARTHUR: *(Humble.)* Oh, its just luck.

WILLY: Luck my foot! You have a future!

(ARTHUR basks in the praise.)

There's just one thing.

ARTHUR: *(Waking up from the praise.)* What?

WILLY: I'm surprised that you didn't catch it.

ARTHUR: Catch what?

WILLY: Its just so obvious! *(Long pause.)* The salesman's death.

ARTHUR: What about it?

WILLY: It should be an accident! *(Pause.)* He should die accidentally.

(ARTHUR droops.)

Oh, come on! Buck up! Its not the end of the world! A twist here or there, and we'll have it! You're very close.

ARTHUR: Look! This is a bad time for me. I'm about to go into production. I'm very vulnerable …

WILLY: I know! That's why, in breaking this to you, I've tried to be sensitive.

ARTHUR: Thanks …

WILLY: You see what I'm saying, don't you? If his death is an accident, we can work in some intrigue. Some suspense!

ARTHUR: *(Something he is unfamiliar with.)* Suspense?

WILLY: If it's an accident, the possibility that it was deliberate immed-iately comes to mind. *(Pause)* What I'm saying is that, if he's going to die anyway, why not make it interesting? Imaginative!

> *(WAITRESS ONE returns with a drink for WILLY. It is in a clear glass with a peculiar coloured liquid. She puts it down, and leaves. WILLY picks it up, absent-mindedly once or twice, and is about to sip it, but it never quite reaches his mouth.)*

If someone is going to kill him, a world of plot possibilities opens up to us. And once the audience sees that someone is after him, we've got them by the balls!

ARTHUR: *(Blandly.)* I don't like you.

WILLY: That doesn't mean we can't work together! I work with all kinds of people I don't like! Look, I'm not crazy about you either. You're a boring person, Art. Look at you! You just sit there. The most exciting adventure could be happening, right under your nose, and you wouldn't know it! You'd miss it. For God's sake, what kind of human being are you? Does your work have to be exactly like you? Have some mercy on the audience, Art!

> *(WAITRESS TWO arrives with WILLY's gin and tonic, notices the ugly looking liquid in the glass in front of him, picks it up and whiffs it, makes an ugly face, and exchanges it with the gin and tonic she has brought. She leaves. WILLY gives ARTHUR a pencil.)*

Here. Take notes!

> *(ARTHUR's confidence is shaken. He takes the pencil.)*

Now the way to build this, is the first time, they try to drug him. Knock him temporarily unconscious. It could be a rival salesman. To beat him to a deal! After this attempt, the audience knows someone is out to get him, but *he* doesn't! Do you understand? *(ARTHUR nods.)* His ignorance is our strength! Now we work it.

(WAITRESS ONE arrives and sees WILLY sipping from the glass.)

WAITRESS ONE: *(Pointing to the glass.)* Where did you get that? Where's that other drink I brought?

WILLY: How do I know? I must have finished it. *(Impatiently.)* Can't you see we're working?

WAITRESS ONE: And you're feeling all right? *(Pause.)* You're not … sleepy?

WILLY: If you're interested, I'm getting an upset stomach from your interrupting.

(WAITRESS ONE looks into his eyes. This begins to make him think. She looks in the direction of WAITRESS TWO with an evil glare.)

WAITRESS ONE: *(Kindly, to ARTHUR.)* A working lunch perhaps? *(Pause.)* How about a piece of pie then? *(Pause.)* Good! I'll bring the knife and fork!

WILLY: *(Suspicious, as he watches her leave.)* You see what I'm saying, Art? Willy is naive! Just like he is in your play now. But then there's a second attempt to remove him, and this second attempt is more extreme. A close shave! A moment that'll have the audience on the edge of their seats. Its a deliberate attempt to injure him. To make sure he's out of the way. This makes him think. He thinks back to what happened earlier. He's beginning to calculate. We're beginning to see an interesting character come to life.

(ARTHUR makes notes between his thoughts.)

ARTHUR: *(Writing.)* Calculate …

WILLY: Am I going too fast?

ARTHUR: No.

WILLY: Past and present come together …

(WAITRESS ONE appears with a knife and fork in her hand. She holds them in her fist, and raises her arm. WAITRESS TWO arrives, sees WAITRESS ONE trying to stab WILLY, and cries out. This makes WILLY turn to see what is happening behind his back. He has to lean to the side as he does so, and WAITRESS ONE

practically falls over him. She misses his back and sticks the knife and fork into the table.)

… in one existential moment!

WAITRESS ONE: Sorry! It's this slippery floor!

(She pulls out a napkin, places it beside ARTHUR, who has remained oblivious, nose buried in his notes, and she pulls the knife and fork, with some effort from the table, and puts them on the napkin.)

I'll just get your pie.

(ARTHUR gives her a smile. WAITRESS ONE exits, giving WAITRESS TWO an evil look over her shoulder. WAITRESS TWO steps forward.)

WILLY: Now that his suspicions are raised, we up the stakes. Now he's looking over his shoulder. He knows that something is going to happen. Here we arrive at the quintessential quintessence of the play!

WAITRESS TWO: Excuse me!

(WILLY jumps out of his chair, and puts a hand on his heart.)

WILLY: You scared the hell out of me!

WAITRESS TWO: Sorry! But I was wondering if you wanted a refill?

WILLY: *(Shoving the drink away.)* We're working. No alcohol. Get me a coffee. I've got to keep a clear head.

(WAITRESS TWO takes his drink away, taking a sip herself on the way out.)

When you're coming back, hum or whistle. So I can hear you coming. Don't sneak up on me!

(WAITRESS TWO exits. WILLY turns to ARTHUR.)

Where were we?

ARTHUR: He's watching over his shoulder.

WILLY: Right! So now he knows someone is after him, but he doesn't know where they're going to strike! Or how! Or how badly they feel they have to hurt him to get him out of the picture. Now you've got everyone in suspense. Including your central character!

ARTHUR: Suspense …

WILLY: Will he get out with his life? Of course he won't!

ARTIIUR: *(Looking up.)* Why not?

WILLY: The title!

ARTHUR: *(Pause.)* Oh right!

WILLY: You've got to kill him! You can't bring an audience into a theatre with a title like that, and not kill him. Or *they'll* kill *you!*

ARTHUR: *(Writing.)* Kill him!

> *(WAITRESS ONE returns with a cup of coffee and puts it down beside WILLY. He hits the roof again.)*

WAITRESS ONE: Are you all right?

WILLY: What did I tell you?

WAITRESS ONE: You wanted a cup of coffee.

WILLY: I told you to hum a tune when you were coming!

WAITRESS ONE: Any particular tune?

WILLY: I don't care what you hum. Sing anything you want!

WAITRESS ONE: We're not that kind of restaurant. We don't have entertainment here.

WILLY: Just don't sneak up on me! That's all I'm saying.

> *(WAITRESS ONE leaves.)*

This'll solve your problem with all your characters being the same. I mean they're all moaning and groaning about their life! I swear, I can't tell them apart. Now if we introduce a killer, there's someone with initiative. It'll change everything. *(Pause.)* You got the title page? *(ARTHUR brings it out.)* We're going to have to change it. *(Pause.)* The title.

ARTHUR: *(Outraged, this is his last refuge.)* I don't want to change it!

WILLY: Look, don't be a baby. All right, we won't change it. We'll just add a word. Write "accidental" in front of it. *(ARTHUR writes.)* This is your insurance of having a hit on your hands. Success is guaranteed now! You're worth a million!

ARTHUR: *(Reading.)* Hmmm.

> *(WAITRESS TWO returns, humming. WILLY is nervous and leans away from her.)*

WAITRESS TWO: Your coffee … Oh, where did that come from?

WILLY: You people are really disorganized around here, aren't you?

WAITRESS TWO: Well, here's a fresh cup. I'll take this away.

> *(She picks up the other cup, and notices the bottom is missing. She looks through it at WILLY, like through a telescope.)*

WILLY: It was full before!

WAITRESS TWO: Oh, we won't charge you for the cup.

> *(She exits. WILLY carefully, with a single finger, pushes away the cup that has been put in front of him.)*

WILLY: *(Nervously.)* Okay, look Art, I've got to go.

> *(WILLY is nervously glancing over his shoulders, as if shoulder-checking while driving.)*

ARTHUR: Just one thing.

WILLY: What?

ARTHUR: He knows someone is trying to hurt him, and he's cautious now with every move he makes. What next?

WILLY: What next?

ARTHUR: *(Looking up.)* Yeah.

WILLY: He has the accident!

ARTHUR: On stage or off?

WILLY: That's up to you. *(Benevolent.)* I don't want to write your script for you. *(He hands ARTHUR a card.)* Give me a call when you finish!

ARTHUR: Thanks.

WILLY: Don't mention it. I hate to see a writer of your calibre remain in obscurity.

> *(WILLY exits furtively. A moment later there is a noise of someone falling down the stairs and a loud scream, off. WAITRESS ONE enters and hurries over to ARTHUR, almost as if hiding behind her work to escape something. She scrubs the side of the table where WILLY sat, as if trying to clean out a spot.)*

ARTHUR: What happened?

WAITRESS ONE: *(Cagey.)* Nothing.

ARTHUR: What was that blood-curdling scream?

WAITRESS ONE: *(Pause.)* There's been an accident. The gentleman who was just with you, tripped over his waitress, and they've fallen down several flights of stairs.

ARTHUR: Oh, my God!

WAITRESS ONE: He won't be bothering you again.

ARTHUR: Dead?

WAITRESS ONE: Both, I'm afraid!

(Long pause.)

ARTHUR: Could I get a cup of coffee?

WAITRESS ONE: Could I suggest our special?

ARTHUR: I've lost my appetite. *(Pause.)* Just coffee.

WAITRESS ONE: Yes, Mr. Miller.

> *(She exits. ARTHUR puts away his script and sits lost in thought. The end.)*

Down to Earth

by Rosemary De Graff

Characters

JIM: In his thirties, with flashbacks to age eleven and his late teens.
FREDA: Jim's mother, in her forties and, later, in her late fifties.
SHARON: Jim's wife, also in her thirties.
GERALD: Jim's father, in his forties.

Setting

The family farm.

(Lights come up, JIM is alone, standing outside looking at the farmhouse and off into the distant fields. On occasion, throughout the play, JIM resumes his narration; these scenes may be set off by lighting changes.)

JIM: *(Narrating.)* Look at this place—I've always pretended it was mine. But it never was—and it never will be. It's Mother's ... those hollyhocks over there, they're Mother's even though Sharon planted them. The house is Mother's too, every last stick of it and the old barn and the chicken coop and all of the fields. They were always Mother's. Even when Dad was still here. And even though Sharon and I live here too, there's never been any doubt about who really owned the place. I think I've known that all my life—ever since I was a kid.

(*FREDA appears. She is feeding the chickens as they cackle noisily around her.*)

FREDA: (*Making clucking sounds of her own.*) Chick, chick, chick! Come on, you fat, stupid, greedy good-for-nothings, waddle over here and stuff yourselves. That's right.

JIM: (*As a boy of eleven.*) Hey, Mom!

FREDA: Hi, Jimmy! Come on, Brownie, you get in here and get your share.

JIM: Brownie looks sick, Mom. Here, let me feed her.

FREDA: Spoiled rotten, that hen. But if she expects me to treat her like a queen, she's got another thing coming!

JIM: Can chickens really think?

FREDA: I swear that one can. Look at her eat, will ya? She's probably figured it out—probably knows if she doesn't shape up, she'll end up as Sunday dinner.

JIM: No, you wouldn't! Not Brownie—you'd never touch Brownie, would you, Mom?

FREDA: Well, if it's left up to your father, she'll die of old age, that's for sure.

JIM: Dad can't kill anything, he told me.

FREDA: It's me that knows it. If it ever came to choosing between us starving to death, and some animal living off the fat of the land, we'd all end up with pretty empty bellies, I can tell you.

JIM: Last year you killed Lucifer for Thanksgiving.

FREDA: It was high time, conceited old buzzard, strutting around the barn like he owned the place.

JIM: And you got rid of old Duke, too.

FREDA: *Old* Duke was right! Your father has no business getting so attached to all these animals, he makes *pets* out of them, for heaven's sake. And as for Duke—he was old and sick. Why, the flies were sitting on him like a blanket, eating him alive. Your Dad refused to have the vet out here, so I had to do something, didn't I?

JIM: But you *shot* him!

FREDA: Most humane way. And I'd do it again if I had to. It's kinder in the long run.

JIM: Will you promise you won't kill Brownie?

FREDA: If she earns her keep and lays lots of eggs, she hasn't got a worry in the world.

JIM: Dad's going to town. He wants to know if you want anything.

FREDA: He's always going to town … One of these times he probably won't come back. Tell him to bring me some sugar for canning. He forgot it the last time.

(FREDA exits.)

JIM: Okay. *(Resumes narrating.)* Dad used to take me with him when he went to town and sometimes we'd sneak into the pool hall before we came home. But Mother always seemed to know. I'd hear them talking sometimes at night before I fell asleep and I'd hear the creak of Dad's chair as he tipped it back against the wall, and I could see the yellow kitchen light spilling like paint into the corner of my room.

(FREDA and GERALD are talking in the farmhouse kitchen.)

GERALD: You know, I've been thinking, Freda.

FREDA: What now?

GERALD: Herb Gifford is retiring this year.

FREDA: Retiring from *what?* Herb Gifford never worked a day in his life.

GERALD: Well, his hardware store's up for sale and I was sorta thinking of buying it …

FREDA: You *what?* Well, you can stop thinking about it right now. I'm not moving into any dumpy little town and working in any hardware store and that's final.

GERALD: You wouldn't have to work. I could hire somebody to help out in the store.

FREDA: And what would I be doing all day long, staring out of the window like a monkey in a zoo? Listen, you're not cut out for living in town anymore than I am, Gerald. You're a farmer through and through, and so am I!

GERALD: I'd like to sell the place, Freda.

FREDA: Sell the place—Never!

GERALD: We could probably get a good price for it. Just think about it, will you?

FREDA: This is our home. We've lived here since the day we got married and we're going to stay right here! Nothing's going to change, everything's going to stay just the way it is!

GERALD: I just don't have the same interest in the place anymore. It's a lot of hard, thankless work and very little reward in the long run.

FREDA: Well, I'm not deserting the place, it's been good to us. Do what you like but just remember one thing, Gerald. You can't sell the place without my say-so and you're never going to get that—*never!*

JIM: *(Narrating.)* Dad gave up and made the best of it, as he did with most things. And everything went on unchanged, the way Mother wanted it. Only one thing was a bit different, though. Dad went into town more often, almost as if he wanted to get away. Sometimes he took me with him, sometimes he didn't ...

(FREDA is seated at the kitchen table across from GERALD. FREDA regards him intently for a long moment.)

FREDA: Well, is it true?

GERALD: Is what true?

FREDA: You know what I'm talking about! That girl in the bank—people have seen you in town, carrying on with her.

GERALD: Carryin' on! What the hell! You shouldn't listen to gossip, Freda, you know that.

FREDA: Where there's smoke, there's fire! They've seen you having lunch with her in the coffee shop, bold as brass, and they've seen her sitting beside you in the truck, and goodness knows what else. Why, Elsa Rathwell could hardly get over here fast enough to tell me. And she wasn't the only one.

GERALD: Do you want Jimmy to hear?

FREDA: Let him find out what kinda father he has—everybody else seems to know.

GERALD: Believe what you like—I don't care.

FREDA: So, it's true, then?

GERALD: I'm not going to lie to you, you wouldn't believe it anyway. You think a man can get along on nothing but working in the field and paying the bills.

FREDA: Other men do!

GERALD: And how would you know? Maybe they're no better than me, maybe *they're* desperately lonely and fed-up, with nothing to live for but more of the same!

FREDA: This has got to stop, Gerald—you and that girl!

GERALD: You stay out of it! You've got Jimmy and the farm, that's all you've ever been interested in, anyway. What more do you want?

FREDA: I want everything to stay the same—just the same as it's always been.

GERALD: I've got a heavy day tomorrow. I'm going to bed.

(He exits.)

FREDA: Gerald! Please don't leave us.

JIM: *(Narrating, moving slowly around the farmyard, remembering.)* That girl in the bank left town and got a transfer to a bank out on the west coast. In the fall, I moved into the city to go to school and came home only on weekends. I began to notice that Dad was getting a lot grayer and a lot quieter. And then, one weekend, I went home as usual, and Mother met me at the bus.

(A younger JIM and FREDA stand awkwardly at the bus depot.)

Where's Dad? Didn't he come with you?

FREDA: He's gone, Jimmy.

JIM: What d'you mean he's gone?

FREDA: He left a couple of days ago.

JIM: But why? Where did he go?

FREDA: He went to Vancouver. At least, that's where he said he was going. That's where *she* is, you know—

JIM: Who?

FREDA: That girl from the bank. They've been corresponding for quite a long time now. Mr. Purvis in the post office said the letters have been coming thick and fast.

JIM: Dad wouldn't do that.

FREDA: Well, he's done it. He's left us high and dry, and there's nothing we can do about it.

JIM: Maybe—maybe he'll come back?

FREDA: Don't count on it. Anyway, I don't want him back. He made his bed, so let him lie in it.

JIM: *(Narrating.)* Mother refused to even mention Dad's name after that. She said that a couple of letters had come but she burned them, unopened. And so, we went on with our lives the best way we could. At university I met a girl named Sharon and we were soon talking about getting married…

(JIM and FREDA are in the farmhouse kitchen.)

FREDA: How could you be thinking of such a thing at your age?

JIM: Why not?

FREDA: You're too young, that's why. Why don't you wait 'til you're older—like your Dad and I did.

JIM: Sure, and look at what happened to you!

FREDA: You can't go! I need you *here!*

JIM: I'll be here.

FREDA: Oh, no, you won't—you'll be with *her.*

JIM: Listen, Mom, Sharon and me—we thought we'd maybe build a little house of our own out here.

FREDA: Where? There's no room.

JIM: There's plenty of room. Well, what about that bush separating our land from the Rathwells? We could tear that down and build there.

FREDA: No. Your father loved that bush. It's been there ever since we moved here.

JIM: Well, Dad's gone now. And you can't expect things to stay the same forever.

FREDA: I don't want another woman on the place. She probably doesn't know a cow from a plough. And don't expect me to teach her.

JIM: Come on, Mom. You're not losing a son, you're gaining a daughter. Remember?

FREDA: I don't want a daughter.

JIM: *(Narrating.)* Well, we got married in spite of Mother. We built our house near the creek, close enough to Mother in case she needed us, yet far enough away so that Sharon and Mother wouldn't get in each other's way. We lived like this for a few years without any of the changes Mother feared coming upon us.

(JIM and SHARON in their kitchen. FREDA enters, out of breath, looking strangely upset.)

Mother! What's the matter?

FREDA: I … I just had to come over. I just had to tell you.

JIM: Tell us what?

FREDA: I always knew this would happen, I always knew.

SHARON: Are you sick, Mother? Would you like to sit down?

FREDA: Sit? How can I sit? The whole world's coming to an end.

JIM: Tell me what's happened, Mother.

FREDA: It's the Rathwells. They're selling their farm.

JIM: I know that. So what?

FREDA: And you know what's going to happen then? A big housing development where their farm is now—streets and houses tearing up the fields and trees. There'll be nothing left. They've already started—they've got their cranes and bulldozers out there right now!

JIM: Calm down, Mom. We still have our farm.

FREDA: Little by little—everything's going—everything's changing—

> *(FREDA begins to have a stroke.)*

JIM: Mother, what is it!

SHARON: *(Crossing to phone.)* I'll phone for the doctor.

FREDA: It's finished … it's all gone!

> *(Lights down then up on JIM.)*

JIM: *(Narrating.)* She'd had a stroke and it was a couple of days before we could see her. The doctor said she'd probably pull through, but she had to be kept perfectly quiet … When I got home from the hospital, two policemen were waiting to see me. They wondered if I could possibly identify the body that had been found in a shallow grave in the bush beside our property. A bulldozer had dug it up only that afternoon. I went with them to look but even before I saw the remains, I knew who it was. His heavy work boots, his wrist-watch … They said he'd been shot in the head. *(Pause.)* Now—how do I tell Mother? How do I tell her my father has been found after all these years? He hadn't gone away at all. How do I tell her about the shallow grave under the poplars where he'd been buried? But maybe I won't have to tell her—maybe she already knows …

> *(Blackout. The end.)*

The Other World of David Wiseman

by Dennis Noble

Characters

DAVID: A fifteen-year-old.
FRANCIE: His Catholic mother.
IZZY: His Jewish father.
WISEMAN and MORELLI: David's grandfathers.

Setting

A bare stage except for four chairs, in two pairs, representing the front and back seats of a car. The car is facing down stage. The back seat area is raised so that when the front seats are occupied, the person in the back is clearly visible to the audience. Actions involving the car, opening the doors, starting the ignition, and steering, for example, can be mimed.

(DAVID enters. He's wearing clothes that are appropriate for a winter day in a northern clime but, like teenagers everywhere, everything is hanging open. DAVID gives every indication that he's going off to an execution. And, in a way, he is. His parents enter a few feet behind him. His mother regards him anxiously as all three cross to the car.)

FRANCIE: David, do up your jacket before you come out in the cold. You catch your death and you'll ruin your whole week.

(They open the car's front doors.)

DAVID: You don't have to drive me, you know. I could just as easily take a taxi.

FRANCIE: Bite your tongue. Our son's going away for a week and we shouldn't drive him to the station? And your scarf. Put on your scarf. Is this how you're going to dress while you're in Banff when I'm not around to look after you?

(DAVID sighs and takes his scarf out of his pocket. He slips it around his neck as they slide into the seats and close the doors.)

IZZY: For an Italian Catholic you sure make a helluva Jewish mother. He's fifteen years old. Will you stop treating him like he's still in diapers? *(To DAVID.)* Did you go to the bathroom before you came out, son?

DAVID: *(Mortified.)* Dad!

IZZY: Did you?

DAVID: *(Sighs.)* Yes.

(IZZY turns the ignition key. He sounds a roar as the car leaps into life and then revs the engine a couple of times until it runs smoothly.)

IZZY: Train station, here we come.

(IZZY shifts into gear and starts off. The three occupants rock backwards as the car picks up speed. DAVID leans forward between his parents. IZZY looks into the rearview mirror.)

What the …!

(He slams on the brakes. The three lean forward as the car skids to a stop. IZZY sounds the squealing brakes. He revs the engine and then turns off the ignition.)

FRANCIE: What's wrong?

IZZY: *(Gesturing to the rear view mirror.)* What's this?

FRANCIE: What's what?

IZZY: Hanging from the rearview mirror?

FRANCIE: A Saint Christopher's medal. What does it look like?

IZZY: Like a Saint Christopher's medal, for chrissakes.

FRANCIE: Don't blaspheme.

(DAVID buries his head in his hands. He's heard it all before.)

IZZY: Do we have to have a Saint Christopher's medal hanging in the car?

FRANCIE: Saint Christopher is the patron saint of travellers, Izzy.

IZZY: But this is a Jewish automobile.

FRANCIE: Only half is Jewish. And he's hanging on the side that's Catholic.

(FRANCIE and IZZY look back at DAVID to see what side of the car he's sitting on. DAVID looks up and quickly shifts to a centre position on the seat.)

IZZY: Our son, the diplomat.

(IZZY looks at the medal again, sighs, turns the key in the ignition and sounds the starter. The car leaps into life. He revs the engine, shifts into gear and drives off. Once the car reaches cruising speed, IZZY fades out the car engine sound, but he continues to steer.)

I found my old ski boots, David. They're on the floor back there.

(FRANCIE and DAVID look down at the floor at DAVID's feet.)

FRANCIE: Cover your ears.

(DAVID makes a gesture of it only, but FRANCIE doesn't notice.)

Don't think you're putting one over on me, Izzy. We agreed we wouldn't try to influence him. We agreed.

IZZY: They're just ski boots, for chrissakes.

FRANCIE: Don't blaspheme. You think I don't see the connection, huh? From father to son? Your ski boots ... your religion?

IZZY: And what about your Saint Christopher? What about that?

FRANCIE: *(Trying to bluff him.)* Saint Christopher is non-denominational.

IZZY: Hah!

FRANCIE: If I had listened to my father all those years ago, I wouldn't be where I am right now ... living in a state of sin. That really upsets him, you know.

IZZY: So what else is new?

FRANCIE: He still blames you for taking me away from the Church.

IZZY: It takes two to tango.

FRANCIE: Cover your ears, David.

(This time DAVID doesn't even bother with the gesture.)

FRANCIE: And now there's his grandson.

IZZY: My father's grandson, too.

FRANCIE: Who has not been baptized a Christian.

IZZY: Who is not Jewish according to Hebrew law.

FRANCIE: How do you think my father, who is very influential in the Italian community, feels about that?

IZZY: And my father who is a founding member of the local chapter of the B'Nai Brith?

FRANCIE: My father, the executive, who has many business interests and is in a position to help David when he comes of age.

IZZY: And my father, the judge, who knows where the skeletons are hidden in this town and can get the right doors opened for him? You hear that, David? Your grandfather, the judge, who can get the right doors opened for you.

FRANCIE: Cover your ears, David.

(A spotlight on DAVID and there is a dramatic lighting change as the past comes to life in DAVID's imagination. All three characters get out of the car, face the audience and make a complete turn. As they turn, DAVID and FRANCIE don gangster-style, 1930s fedoras and IZZY sticks a toothpick in his mouth. When they face the audience again they have assumed new roles: DAVID has become his paternal grandfather, Sol WISEMAN, and FRANCIE has become David's maternal grandfather, Giuseppe MORELLI. IZZY remains himself, but at a much younger age. The lighting returns to normal. MORELLI and WISEMAN eye each other warily. IZZY lounges against the car, an insolent grin on his face.)

MORELLI: 'Eh! 'Eh!

(He waves WISEMAN closer. WISEMAN advances cautiously.)

Sol Wiseman, I've just-a put out a contract on your son, Izzy.

(IZZY bolts upright. WISEMAN holds up a cautionary hand. IZZY settles down.)

WISEMAN: Let's not beat around the bush, Giuseppi Morelli. How much is the contract for?

MORELLI: Fifty thousand-a dollars.

WISEMAN: You put out a contract on my son for fifty thousand? I take offense, Morelli. Fifty thousand is an insult.

(WISEMAN mimes pulling out a tommygun from under his coat.)

MORELLI: 'Eh! Fifty thousand is all your son is worth.

(MORELLI pulls out his own tommygun. The two men maneuver for position and, making machine-gun sounds, blast away at each other. IZZY leaps up onto the car. The two men ignore him as he scurries to get out of the line of fire. The shooting stops.)

WISEMAN: I remind you, Morelli, that he is a married man. Think of the embarrassment such a paltry sum would bring to his widow, your daughter.

(WISEMAN lets loose with a short blast and then ducks behind the car.)

MORELLI: You have a point-a, Wiseman. Sixty thousand.

(MORELLI peeks around a fender and sprays bullets in the vicinity of WISEMAN. IZZY dances on the car to avoid getting hit.)

WISEMAN: I also remind you, Morelli, that out of this union has been produced a male child. Surely a man who has given you a grandson is worth more than sixty thousand.

MORELLI: And I remind-a you that my grandson has-a been circumcised.

WISEMAN: But not by a Rabbi.

MORELLI: *(Acknowledging the distinction.)* Seventy thousand.

(MORELLI grabs a car seat as a shield and drags it off to one side. IZZY watches in dismay. He sits on one and holds tightly onto the other two.)

WISEMAN: Seventy thousand? For your only grandchild?

(WISEMAN sprays the room. He rushes around the car. No MORELLI. MORELLI speaks and WISEMAN ducks instinctively.)

MORELLI: 'Eh, Wiseman. You must-a understand. I'm not a rich man.

(WISEMAN grabs a car seat as a shield. But IZZY has no intention of letting any more of his sanctuary be dismantled. He grabs it back. They tug on it. WISEMAN shows IZZY his tommygun. IZZY lets go and hides behind the car.)

WISEMAN: For the child, Morelli. Your grandson. How can you deny little David?

MORELLI: Little David has-a not yet decided to become a Catholic.

WISEMAN: That is true, Morelli. But neither has he decided to become a Jew.

MORELLI: Eighty thousand.

WISEMAN: The figure I had in mind was a hundred and twenty-five thousand. Now that is a contract a man can live with.

MORELLI: Tell-a you what, Wiseman. After the contract has-a been carried out, you use-a your influence to have David become a Catholic, and I'll go for … ninety thousand, tops.

WISEMAN: It's an attractive offer, Morelli, but impractical. Whoever heard of a Catholic named Wiseman?

MORELLI: That's another thing, Wiseman. I want David to change-a his name.

WISEMAN: Change his name? What's the matter, Morelli? Even your Michelangelo had a statue named David.

(WISEMAN tries to work his way closer to MORELLI. He starts to run from behind the chair. MORELLI steps out to shoot but finds he's out of ammunition. He throws the gun aside and blasts WISEMAN with a line from Vesti La Giubba from Pagliacci.)

MORELLI: *(Sings.)* Vesti la giubba e la faccia infarina.

(WISEMAN cringes. MORELLI leaps for cover. WISEMAN decides to meet fire with fire. He, too, throws aside his gun and breaks out in song.)

WISEMAN: Hava nagila, hava nagila, hava nagila, venismecha.

(MORELLI cringes. WISEMAN leaps for cover. MORELLI takes off the gloves. He attacks with Pagliacci again. But this time he doesn't quit. WISEMAN counter-attacks with Hava Nagila. The intensity and volume grow as they stand toe to toe and hammer the words out. Finally, the assault is too much for MORELLI. He jumps for cover. WISEMAN follows suit.)

MORELLI: Alright! Enough! We'll split-a the difference. A hundred thousand.

WISEMAN: Of course there's my fee, and the cost of the legal documents. Stamps. Consideration. Good will. And the funeral. Don't forget the funeral. A hundred and twenty thousand.

MORELLI: A hundred and ten. My final offer.

WISEMAN: Alright. But only because you're family.

(They both come out of hiding. They stretch out their arms to each other, ready to embrace.)

MORELLI: 'Eh!

WISEMAN: Ahhhh!

MORELLI: Sol-a!

WISEMAN: Giuseppi!

> *(They embrace and pat each other on the back affectionately. Then they turn as one and regard IZZY proprietorally. WISEMAN beckons to IZZY. IZZY shuffles nervously but remains where he is. Both WISMAN and MORELLI beckon to IZZY. Cautiously, IZZY steps towards them. Then he waits. WISEMAN and MORELLI take aim at IZZY and blast him with a couple of lines from Vesti La Guibba.)*

WISEMAN and MORELLI: *(Singing.)* Ri-di, Pa-gliac-cio, sul tuo a-mo-re infran-to! Ri-di del duol che t'av-ve-le-na il cor!

> *(IZZY backs away, spins around and runs for his life. He jumps into the front seat of the car and beats on the horn. A spotlight hits IZZY. In a dramatic lighting change, WISEMAN and MORELLI sweep the chairs up and, in a continuous motion, reform the car, remove their fedoras and assume their original seats in the car as DAVID and FRANCIE. The lighting returns to normal. IZZY, still sounding the horn, hits the brakes and they are all thrown forward.)*

FRANCIE: Izzy! You could have thrown me through the windshield.

IZZY: *(Shouts out the window.)* Sunday driver! Oh, here we are. The train station.

FRANCIE: Already?

> *(IZZY pulls into the station.)*

DAVID: You can just let me off here, okay? I can find my way.

FRANCIE: *(Shakily.)* Oh, dear.

IZZY: Now don't get all weepy on us.

DAVID: You don't have to come in, you know.

FRANCIE: I don't know why I agreed to this trip. He's never been on skis in his life.

IZZY: Going skiing in Banff is like a rite of passage, Francie. It's a part of growing up.

> *(They climb out of the car and close the doors.)*

FRANCIE: Let him grow up next year. This year he should stay my little boy.

DAVID: *(Mortified.)* Oh, Mom!

IZZY: All the more reason he should go. So that when he comes back, he comes back a man—ready to take on his responsibilities, his obligations, his Bar Mitzvah.

(They start toward the exit.)

FRANCIE: His confirmation.

IZZY: That's for our son to decide. Right, David? When you come back, we expect answers. And not just any answers. The right answers.

DAVID: *(Dispiritedly.)* Sure, Dad.

FRANCIE: No pressuring, Izzy.

IZZY: Who's pressuring? Just some advice for the apple of my eye. You're going to Banff, David, circumcised. I expect you to come back in the same condition.

FRANCIE: Izzy! That's not fair. Don't listen to him, David.

DAVID: I guess we can say good-by here. It's kind of crowded by the train.

FRANCIE: Don't be silly. We want to make sure that you get on safely.

DAVID: What can happen between here and the train?

FRANCIE: Oh, look. They're loading already. Come on, David.

(FRANCIE beckons. DAVID sighs and walks past her to exit. He pauses momentarily, looking off, reluctant to leave, knowing full well that his parents are going to embarrass him in front of his friends. His parents watch him, concerned.)

Poor David, he's going to be lost without us.

IZZY: Don't let on that you're worried, Francie. We've got to be brave for his sake. We don't want to embarrass him in front of his friends.

FRANCIE: *(Loudly.)* And underwear, David. Remember, a clean pair every day.

(DAVID clasps his hand to his brow in despair and exits. His parents follow after him.)

IZZY: You've got my number at work, David. Any problems, just give me a call.

FRANCIE: What's wrong with calling you at home?

IZZY: I'm not at home in the daytime.

FRANCIE: So he can call you at home at night. You hear, David? Call your father at night.

(They're off. The end.)

Contributors

VALORIE BUNCE'S play, *Questions About Cleopatra*, was produced at the 1990 Fringe Festival and her full length play, *Bitter Sweet*, played in New York City off- off-Broadway. Currently she attends university and makes time for writing when she can.

RICK CHAFE is an educator and playwright whose work includes many fringe productions. He has worked with young playwrights in the schools as both a dramaturge and a director. His most recent plays are *Zac and Speth, Player Pool* and *Six Times a Day.*

As a writer and actor, BEVERLEY COOPER has worked in film, TV, radio and theatre. She is a contributor to *Adventures for (Big) Girls* (Blizzard, 1993) and has a son named Will.

COLLEEN CURRAN is a Montreal Playwright and Co-Artistic Director of the Triumvirate Theatre Company. Her plays include *Cake-Walk, Sacred Hearts, El Clavadista, Local Talent* and *Ceili House.* Her most recent play is *Villa Eden.*

ROSEMARY DE GRAFF has been writing for radio and TV for a number of years. Her plays have been staged by such theatres as Actor's Show-case, Popular Theatre Alliance and Agassiz Theatre.

Co-founder of Green Thumb Theatre, DENNIS FOON was its artistic director for twelve years, where he directed, wrote or dramaturged many award winning productions. His plays include *New Canadian Kid, Invisible Kids* (British Theatre Award), *Mirror Game* (Blizzard, 1992), *Skin* (Chalmers Award) and *Seesaw* (Blizzard, 1993).

NORM FOSTER is one of Canada's most produced and prolific playwrights. He is best known for his play *The Melville Boys* which has been performed all across Canada and which won the Los Angeles Drama-Logue Critics Award in 1988.

DAVID GILLIES is an actor and writer who has appeared in movies, television and on radio as well as on the stages of theatres across Canada. His plays include *A Prairie Boy's Winter*, *Pinnochio*, *You Can Do It If You Try*, *Everyday Heroes*, and *There Is No Shame*.

WILLIAM HARRAR lives and works on farms in Western Manitoba. He has written several plays for the stage including *Bolshi Bash*, as well as having five radio plays produced by CBC. He's most recent play, *Shooting J.J.*, dramatizes the J.J. Harper incident.

Writer and playwright, PHIL MCBURNEY'S short fiction has been published and anthologized in Canada and the United States. His radio drama *The Rally* will be aired on the CBC in 1994.

DOUG MELNYK is a multi-media artist whose work is normally text based. A number of his videos are in public collections at the National Gallery of Canada, The Museum of Modern Art in New York and the Winnipeg Art Gallery. His book, *Naked Croquet*, was published in 1987.

NICK MITCHELL'S play *Tin Can Cathedral* premièred at Prairie Theatre Exchange in the fall of 1993. He was writer in residence at St. Andrew's College at the Univeristy of Manitoba from 1990 to 1991.

ELISE MOORE, nominated by the Canadian Authors Association for the Air Canada Award for most promising author under the age of thirty, has, at age eighteen, had her first full-length play professionally produced. *Live With It*, (Blizzard, 1994) is about the murder of Joe Orton.

GREG NELSON'S play *Castrato* (Blizzard, 1993) won the 1992 Canadian National Playwrighting Competition and the 1993 Sterling Award. His most recent plays are *Spirit Rustler* and *The Cure*. He currently lives in Saskatoon.

DENNIS NOBLE is an associate professor of Theatre and Drama at the University of Winnipeg. A recipient of many American awards, his latest plays include *R.A.T.S.* and *The Rehearsal*.

DEBORAH O'NEIL'S most recent plays include *#1 Gem*, *Worm Moon*, and a one-act play, *Virgins Don't Eavesdrop*.

MARK OWEN is the Artistic Director of 3$bill Theatre in New York City. His full length play, *Perth Road*, was produced in Toronto and New York City at the Circle Rep Lab. His new play, *Evidence We Were Here,* was produced in New York City last year and featured Joe Mantello.

ELLEN PETERSON supports herself by writing, acting, teaching and working in a greenhouse. She commutes regularly between her home in Narol and Winnipeg.

SHARON POLLOCK has won numerous awards for her work, including two Governor General's Awards for her plays *Blood Relations* and *Doc,* as well as winning the Canadian-Australian Literary Award for her contributions to Canadian writing. *Saucy Jack* is Sharon Pollock's most recent play.

LORA SCHROEDER and TANNIS KOWALCHUK both live and work in Winnipeg. They are best known for their plays *Jumping Off the CN Tower*, *The Journey of the Dragon Boy*, and *The Grimm Sisters*. Tannis is currently working with Primus Theatre and Lora is freelancing as an actor and writer.

REBECCA SHAW and ANDREW WREGGITT have written *Ms. Lone Pine*, *The Wild Guys* (Blizzard, 1994) which won the National Playwrighting Competition and *Two-Step*. They are currently at work on a new play.

CAROL SHIELDS, author of the acclaimed novels *The Stone Diaries* and *The Republic of Love*, has written two plays, *Departures and Arrivals* (Blizzard, 1991) and *Thirteen Hands* (Blizzard, 1993).

DONN SHORT'S first play, *Good-bye and Keep Cold*, was the winner of the 1993 duMaurier Arts National Canadian One-Act Play Competition. *Playing With Angels* is a finalist in the Actors Theatre of Louisville's 1993 National Ten-Minute Play Competition, and re-written as a longer piece, received a special prize at the 1993 National Canadian Play Competition.

An actor, writer and director, GUILLERMO VERDECCHIA lives with his partner, Tamsin, and their daughter, Anaïs, in Vancouver. Though now older and wiser, he has still not overcome the compulsion to write cheap satire.

DAVID WIDDICOMBE has been Playwright-in-Residence at the Factory Theatre in Toronto and has written several plays for CBC Radio Drama. His other stage plays include *Dinosaur Dreams, Swamp Baby and Other Tales* and *The River Lady*.

Currently Director of Writing at the Banff Centre for the Arts, RACHEL WYATT has written countless dramas for radio for both the CBC and BBC. Her stage plays have been produced by the Tarragon Theatre in Toronto and she has to her writing credit several novels and short stories, published in many literary journals.

The publishers wish to extend their thanks and gratitude to M.A.P. and A.T.P. for providing some of the original manuscripts to this anthology.